The Men I've Almost Dated

Lucretia Ackfield

This is a First Edition

First published 2016 by Lucretia's Words

PO Box 5594 Stafford Heights, Queensland 4053 Australia

Email: lucretia@lucretiaswords.com

ISBN: 9780994569608 (paperback)

ISBN: 9780994569615 (eBook)

Cover illustration and design: Hannah Munster,

Munster Design & Print

www.munsterdesignandprint.com

Author photograph: Lauren Jordan,

www.laurenjordan.com.au

For all the women who still
believe in love.
Don't give up.

Table of Contents

PART 1
The Wedding, the Car Park and Other Realisations

Lucretia Ackfield

The Wedding

Grandma sobbed throughout my wedding and I don't mean quiet whimpers and sniffles. Her cries filled the gaps, reached a crescendo between the vows and carried over our words. 'She's just over-emotional because of her stroke,' Mum explained afterwards. I took her point but it seemed like a lot of crying for a 'happy' occasion.

I'd had my own slightly hysterical meltdown when the wedding cars arrived two hours earlier. Everything else had been going according to plan. Mostly. I'd contracted infections in both ears and my throat three days before but the antibiotics and a generous slathering of Vaseline every night had mitigated a possible red nose situation. Thank God! Meanwhile, although the fumes at the salon almost made me pass out (and there were probably 100 pins in my hair) the curls and sweet semi-circle of flowers on top of my head were just right. The photographer arrived on time – which was good. Then we realised one of the floral lapel pins was missing so my soon-to-be brother-in-law William had to dash back to the florist. But he made it back on time.

It was the usual chaos associated with a major family event and I was fine, I really was, until the wedding cars arrived.

They edged slowly, funeral-like, down my parents' driveway and triggered my immediate panic and a swift exit to the bathroom. Wanda my head bridesmaid found me there a short time later, perched on the white storage box, holding my head in my hands, and rocking back and forth like a mentally-deranged person.

'What am I doing? I can't do this. What am I doing? This is crazy. What am I doing? I can't do this.' I wasn't holding it together very well.

'What's going on?' Wanda demanded. She was a straightforward person and it seemed a fair question under the circumstances.

'What am I doing?' I asked. 'I can't do this.'

She gave me a hard look then said, 'Lucretia, do you think I'd let you do this if I didn't think it was right?'

The Men I've Almost Dated

And that was that.

I'd met Wanda in my first week at university and she had a lot of common sense. She would have told me if I was doing something stupid and her perspective was enough to shake me out of my panic. Of course I was doing the right thing.

Thirty minutes later Dad was holding my hand as the car approached the New Farm Park rotunda. We didn't say much and I was calm and regally bride-like as I stepped out onto the footpath. Then my garter leapt for freedom, landing near my feet like a frilly blue and white anklet. Everyone thought that was hilarious. I can still, to this day, remember the sound of Auntie Brenda cackling away at the spectacle.

Years later, someone told me it was bad luck if your garter fell off at your wedding. But I didn't know that at the time. I was just embarrassed because my perfect entrance would have involved exiting the car gracefully and gliding effortlessly up the path towards the rotunda, not fumbling around at my feet and hiking a piece of elastic back up under my skirt.

Lucretia Ackfield

I eventually made it up the aisle and minutes later two Japanese tourists settled in to watch the ceremony from a nearby park bench. It was unnerving to have those uninvited guests studying me. What were they thinking about me - a young Australian girl in an ivory and gold satin dress with layers of tulle that would later prove enticing to the colony of tiny black bugs living in the surrounding rose gardens?

As the celebrant began the ceremony, I noticed the best man had tears in his eyes. So did Daniel (the groom). I was happy but didn't cry. I felt a little detached, like I was physically present but observing at the same time.

Less than 15 minutes later I was married to my sweetheart, Daniel. It was 10 days before my 23rd birthday. We made promises to love each other forever under a darkening sky that later erupted with torrential rain. I loved Daniel very much. He was my rock and the man everyone loved. He was a blonde, good-looking Aussie bloke; a combination of surfie and rev-head with a gift for making people laugh and a talent for

The Men I've Almost Dated

fixing things. He was safe, secure, loving and reliable. He was my everything.

Ten years and two days after my wedding, I walked out my front door, got into my car and drove to my parents' house. I had become something different from that innocent 22-year-old girl. I'd been in a relationship with Daniel for 15 years but now I was almost 32 and suddenly single.

I was naïve and I didn't have a plan.

It was going to be a bumpy ride.

Lucretia Ackfield

Under the Influence of 30

Leaving Daniel wasn't a decision I made overnight. It actually took years to reach the point of no return with my marriage but you could say turning thirty was a strong influencing factor.

The big 3-0 can have a strong impact on women. For some, it's when we first hear the sustained tick, tick, tick of the biological clock. Often it's also when we fully step into our skins and develop a greater understanding of who we are and what we want from life. We aren't kids in our 20s anymore and it's time to 'get real'.

I started changing as I approached 30 and, although everyone loved Daniel, I stopped loving him. Or at least, I no longer loved him in the same way. The realisation was a massive shock for me. It would be an even bigger shock for my friends and family. Devastated might be a better description for how some of them felt.

The Men I've Almost Dated

I can't tell you exactly when I fell out of love. It was more a slow erosion over time marked by me changing and wanting a different life. Daniel didn't want to change. He was still the man I married and I guess he thought that should be enough. Maybe it should've been.

He was my first serious boyfriend and in my early 20s he was exactly what I wanted. But once I started changing, I couldn't change back.

I didn't leave Daniel for someone else. But I did think about having an affair and that's when my life really began to unravel. That I could even consider having sex with another man was inconceivable and shook me to the core.

In March 2003 my life was in transition and I'd left a full-time, permanent job to escape a toxic work environment. I was turning into a jaded and bitter version of my former self and radical action was needed. For a woman who didn't take risks, walking away from job security was a very big deal.

By the time I met Simon in July – he was a new colleague in a government department - I was beginning to feel the first stirrings of a real inner self-confidence. My career risks were leading to amazing opportunities and I felt stronger and more energised. I wasn't being as sensible as I used to be. I'd spent most of my life wanting to be taken seriously and wanted people to know I was smart, reliable and hard-working. I'd been the queen of structured suits and sensible shoes. No one would have ever described me as frivolous.

But my new confidence led to changes in how I thought about myself and how I looked on the outside. Now, I wasn't quite so sensible anymore. I started wearing clothes that actually hugged my shape instead of hiding it and my stilettoes were geared for serious fun not serious stuffiness.

Then I met Simon. He was married, older, jaded and the complete opposite of Daniel in every possible way. We were sent on a photo shoot together and I wasn't sure what to make of him at first. My default behaviour in most situations is to be light and chatty, whereas he was quiet, thoughtful and introverted.

On the way back in the car we started to really talk and discovered a shared worldview about many topics including politics and Indigenous affairs, two issues I was very passionate about. It felt like we were in sync.

Daniel was never into politics and his leanings were generally far more conservative than mine.

Simon and I talked about things we both cared about. Then it changed from being an interesting and invigorating exchange of ideas to something else entirely.

We were standing in the car park around 4pm, unpacking the car and talking about marriage and children. 'I would've liked more kids,' he said, 'but my wife didn't want anymore.'

'I'd have children with you in a second,' I thought.

In that moment, in that car park, my world stopped and the nice secure life I knew ended.

I'd never felt that way with Daniel. We'd started talking about kids but I'd never felt compelled to do anything more about it. We also had very different perspectives about how they should be raised and what my role would be. Daniel preferred a more traditional set-up while my values demanded something more modern. As a long-time feminist, his expectation I should stay home full-time until the children went to school was offensive, particularly when any interruption to his career was apparently not an option.

The car park incident rocked me to the core and, as I drove home that night, my brain whirled this way and that. Why on earth would I think such a thing about a complete stranger? It didn't make sense. I was clearly a terrible and disloyal person.

Over the coming months, Simon and I had coffee occasionally, worked together and, although we both considered taking it further, it remained a flirtation. But the feelings and thoughts he triggered in me wouldn't disappear no matter how much I fought them. I hated myself. How could I think of betraying the wonderful man who had been at my side for so long?

I didn't understand who I was anymore and began questioning everything in my life – my work, who I was, my relationship with Daniel. Simon had opened a door and all kinds of unstoppable thoughts and feelings began flooding through.

The intermittent depression and anxiety of my twenties reared their ugly heads again and I descended into self-loathing on an epic scale. I wanted to scratch my skin off from the inside. I cried a lot. I would even wake up sobbing in the early hours of the morning. I was constantly distracted and called in sick several times when I just couldn't cope with leaving the house. This went on for months.

How could I love one good man but want to rip the clothes off another? Who was this femme fatale I had turned into?

A few months after the 'car park incident', on yet another sick day, I found myself running my finger down a list of psychologists and counselors in the phone directory. I picked a random number and the woman on the other end of the phone line said, 'Yes, I can see you this afternoon.' By the time I walked through her door, I was desperate for help.

The session changed my life.

Raina was in her late 40s with dark wiry hair and a kind smile. She ran a small counseling practice in inner-city Brisbane and, when she asked me why I had come to see her, the floodgates opened.

She sat quietly while I talked, cried and rambled for around 30 minutes. I laid my soul bare. I wasn't looking for absolution. I just wanted to understand who I'd become. When I finally ran out of words, Raina rose from her chair, picked up a thick black marker from a side table and moved to a white flip chart standing in the corner.

She drew a large oval shape with a line down the middle.

'There are two sides of you,' she said.

'This 'new you', the one you feel is out of control, is a side that's been repressed for a very long time. Simon has triggered her appearance and she's here to stay. There will eventually be a balance between the old and new you,' she said. 'But this is who you are. It isn't actually about Simon,' she added. 'It's what he represents in your mind.'

Looking back now I think Simon triggered feelings of freedom, change and possibilities; a hint of a life that could be so very different from the one I was leading. But my emotional upheaval was too rampant

The Men I've Almost Dated

for me to understand what was really happening. Meanwhile, Raina's insights about my situation were enlightening and terrifying at the same time - this 'new me' was part of me. I'd spent most of my life trying to be the 'good' girl but now the other side of me, the one who wanted to run amok and turn everything upside down, had taken over.

I left the session feeling calmer but still spent the next two years trying to run away from the 'new me'. The alternative, to throw away my comfortable life and a 'good man', was too cruel. My heart wanted change but I stayed married. I couldn't face myself yet.

I wanted to go out and experience new things so I asked Daniel to come out with me. But he preferred to stay home watching the football or renovating the house. I didn't want to stay in. My parents had a better social life than we did.

So I went out without him. My friend Jamie's marriage was also breaking down and we'd often meet at the local pub after work where the entertainment manager, a long-haired sleazy guy called Ken, was happy to provide free drinks. Jamie was tall, blonde and good-looking and I'm pretty sure Ken was hoping to get her into bed during a weak moment. But that was never going to happen. We appreciated the free alcohol and I was on a mission to change my tee-totaling habits. You would find us at the bar at least once or twice a week, talking intently, occasionally getting teary, and trying to solve the confusion, dysfunction and unhappiness of our lives.

During that time I also found myself drawn to other women who were going through similar upheavals: women having affairs, women who had just left their husbands and women who were thinking about leaving. We would always find each other, at parties, in the workplace and everywhere else. Perhaps it was just the law of attraction; what you put out you also receive. I'd meet a complete stranger at a party, one of us would make an off-hand comment and in that moment we'd see that same confusion, fear and exhilaration reflected in each other and our words would come tumbling out.

We may have been strangers but we were experiencing the same things and were all

around the same age. It was as if our 30th
birthdays made us turn a corner and
suddenly we didn't recognise where we
were anymore.

We looked at our lives and asked, 'Is this
what I want?'

'Is this who I am?'

'What the fuck is going on?'

Lucretia Ackfield

The Smell of Sex

I also began to realise around this time that men could innately smell when a woman was back on the market, sometimes even before she was aware of it herself. I knew this because, as my marriage started breaking down, the 'new me' began attracting a lot of masculine attention.

I found myself being flirted with at work, at the shops, at clubs and pubs, and everywhere else. It was a novel and completely new experience.

I actually believe they could smell sex on me. Like the proverbial dogs scampering after a bitch on heat, men would sniff me out and behave in the most bizarre ways to attract my attention. Male colleagues and associates would find an excuse to chat to me, touch my hair unexpectedly and comment on my appearance. One even opened my car door and kissed me on the cheek after a work meeting...so not appropriate!

The Men I've Almost Dated

Men with long-term partners began greeting me with hugs and hands that lingered just a little too long on my hips. I've always thought cradling a woman's hipbones connotes intimacy and is something only a lover or potential lover should do. I'm sure those men were thinking exactly the same thing.

Late one afternoon I returned from a walk and found Daniel and his friend Sam chatting in the garage. I'd been caught in the rain and Sam chose to comment on this by reaching over, dragging his finger slowly up my arm and saying, 'You're all wet.'

I don't think he was talking about the water on my skin.

Bizarrely, Daniel was standing right beside me but I don't think he even registered the undercurrent. I often wondered if he noticed the attention I was attracting and part of me felt like he didn't see me as a sexual woman at all.

As time passed, men exhibiting poor judgement and low impulse control became commonplace in my world. I didn't consciously encourage the behaviour. I just thought men were behaving weirdly. I was pretty naïve and inexperienced. Daniel was the first and only man I'd been intimate with so I was ill-equipped to deal with the attention. It was the obviousness of their behaviour that most perplexed me and Peter was just another example of very unsubtle male weirdness at the time.

I was chatting to some colleagues at a work function when I noticed him standing nearby.

'Oh, hi. It's Peter isn't it?' I said. 'I think we met at the pub a couple of weeks ago for drinks with Anna? You were there with your partner, Candace.' At this point, Peter reached across in front of two other people, lightly grabbed my upper arm and said laughingly while intently holding eye contact, 'Oh, don't call her that. She's not really my partner.'

My first thought was, 'What the hell is he doing? Anna said he's been dating Candace for years and they're moving in together!'

These types of incidents became the rule, not the exception.

And I hated all the attention didn't I? I wanted to slap their faces and tell them all to fuck off…right? Honestly, no. I'm ashamed to admit that while I was tormenting myself about whether to leave my marriage, another part of me loved the attention I was receiving. I didn't really know what to do with it, why it was happening or how to manage it. But yes, part of me loved it because it reminded me I was a desirable woman. Perhaps it was the Universe telling me that, even if I left my marriage, there would still be men in my future.

It was a difficult time. I needed to leave part of me behind, but I wasn't quite ready to step off the precipice into the future. I became increasingly reckless with my emotions and behaviour. I was just a little bit out of control. I drank too much, stayed out late, talked too much and generally attracted a lot of attention.

Some friends in similar situations had affairs, often with deeply scarring results: ugly confrontations with partners, unwanted pregnancies, terminations, guilt, fear, exhilaration and adrenalin. A heady cocktail of sex was seeping through every pore of our bodies and into relationships where it had never existed before.

Lucretia Ackfield

My life was changing into something I didn't recognise. The smell of sex was just the start.

The Men I've Almost Dated

The Departure Lounge

Deciding to leave Daniel was incredibly difficult and I asked so many people, 'How will I know what to do? What should I do?'

The questions would ring in my head morning, noon and night; like tinnitus, I just couldn't drown them out. Alcohol and denial didn't work. Laughing it off didn't work either. Only I could make the decision but I still sought guidance from almost everyone.

My friend Jamie, who by this stage had left her destructive marriage, gave me some wonderful advice. 'Stop pressuring yourself,' she said as we sat at our local pub one night. We were drinking wine as usual and attempting to drown our sorrows. 'When the time is right you'll know what to do.'

It sounded simple but I found it so very difficult. I'd never been great at just parking something in my brain and letting time sort it out. So I tormented myself about what I should do and how it would impact other people - hurt them, make them disappointed or prove them right.

I almost went mad. I'm surprised I managed to hold down jobs while I was in that place of constant confusion and indecision.

When it became clear our relationship was in serious trouble, Daniel and I tried to pull it back from the brink by visiting Raina my counselor. But she put Daniel offside in the first session.

'Would you love Lucretia as much if she was 100kg heavier?' she asked.

'Of course,' he said indignantly. For him it was a dumb question because when you loved someone, you loved all of them, no matter what.

Raina laughed aloud and clearly didn't believe him. She'd been through a divorce of her own and was jaded about men and marriage. Daniel wasn't impressed with her attitude and it was obvious Raina wasn't the right person to help heal our marriage. She'd been great at helping me understand the changes I was experiencing but she was too tainted by her own break-up to help us.

The Men I've Almost Dated

Daniel and I moved on to a male counselor after that, but it didn't really help. We kept falling into the same patterns. I wanted him to surprise me and do something different.

'Let's go rock climbing or abseiling,' I'd suggest.

He kept taking me out for dinner, just like he always had.

On the surface it was such a small thing. But it was a symptom of our separateness. We weren't on the same page. I needed our relationship to grow. I wanted to grow. I wanted to explore and expand but he wanted things to stay the same. We just weren't hearing each other any more.

Our relationship limped onwards.

In October 2005 we celebrated our 10-year wedding anniversary with a weekend getaway in the Sunshine Coast hinterland. Daniel organised a romantic cabin for us to stay in and we dined in an intimate restaurant conducive to holding hands and rekindling our relationship. But in the cabin where we stayed, the sex was nondescript. I wanted desperately to connect but I just couldn't feel anything anymore.

Lucretia Ackfield

We returned home on Sunday night and halfway through watching some mind-numbing program on television I found myself rising from the couch as tears began filling my eyes. Then I simply walked to the bedroom and began packing a bag. I couldn't stop crying. I remember holding onto the towel rail in the bathroom minutes later, doubled-over and sobbing, while Daniel stood in the doorway and asked with panic in his voice, 'What are you doing? Where are you going?'

'I'm sorry. I have to go,' I said. 'I can't do this anymore.'

In less than 15 minutes I was in my car, driving to my parents' house. I knew I'd done the right thing. It was time. Jamie was right; when you know, you know. But I was wretched with grief.

Dad was travelling for work but sent his advice by email the next day. 'If Lucretia doesn't want children with Daniel then she should just call it quits,' he wrote.

I guess everyone has their own way of making sense of relationships. Dad, like so many men of his generation, saw these issues in impervious blacks and blinding

The Men I've Almost Dated

whites. Having children and a family was how he made sense of it all. Life may be simpler that way but my brain never conformed to that model. The question of children was the least of our problems.

Daniel and I began a trial separation and had more counseling. But it didn't work. Our 'dates' during that time felt forced and when I tried flirting with him, my words sounded unconvincing even to my ears.

He still wanted to take me out for dinner. I still wanted to go rock climbing.

On the Australia Day weekend in late January, we found ourselves lying in bed together, quietly breathing and staring at the ceiling in the house we'd shared for so long. We'd spent the afternoon just hanging out before lying down for an afternoon nap. It was almost four months since I'd moved out.

We lay side-by-side for a long time and then came the moment when we both realised it was over. We had done everything we could but it was done. Nothing was said, but we knew it in our hearts.

Lucretia Ackfield

There was no acrimony and the settlement was straightforward. I felt guilty for leaving and didn't fight very hard over the financial side of things. My solicitor was frustrated about that. 'Women often give away more than they should in these situations,' she said. 'You're too nice or, if you've been the one to walk away, you just feel too guilty to fight.'

The solicitor was right. I did feel guilty and I would feel guilty for years to come.

When the courts officially ended my marriage, a large part of my life was over. I was at the airport of life and about to leave the departure lounge. But even as I boarded the plane I didn't know my destination.

Surviving the Impact

A lot of people will tell you that marriage is too easy to get out of 'these days'. 'People don't work at things anymore and they don't take it seriously enough. That's why the divorce rate is so high,' they say.

But I don't believe that for a second. Most people don't give up on their marriages lightly or quickly. Rarely do we simply wake up one morning, without any forethought or warning, and decide to call it quits.

I didn't feel joy when I left my marriage. Even when I knew it was for the best and we both needed to let go of each other, it was still awful, painful, uncomfortable and gut-wrenchingly difficult. And then, just when I thought I was fine, the final divorce papers arrived and I spun out of control again. So I started an affair with a married man. Clearly my self-esteem wasn't riding high.

I'd been rushing around my back yard a few weeks earlier, running late as usual, when I looked up and saw him. Him being

Barry, and he was perched on my neighbour's roof. He was conducting a building inspection and it felt like he'd been watching me for a while.

We quietly observed each other for a moment or two before I broke the silence.

'Hi,' I said.

'Hi,' he said.

Then I went back inside and got on with my day.

Our affair started the day after my divorce papers arrived. He'd been married for decades and said I was only his second indiscretion. I chose to believe him. Barry was 10 years older and, when he first removed his cap, I was taken aback for a moment by his grey hair and balding head. But still I proceeded. I needed to feel something, anything. I needed to feel wanted.

Did I think about his wife? I guess so. But I rationalised that it was his relationship not mine. It was his choice. I guess that makes me sound cold and it's not part of my life I'm proud of. But I wasn't thinking too straight. Over the following decade I'd find married and otherwise attached men would frequently proposition and flirt with me but I would always decline. I wanted someone who was mine, not another woman's leftovers.

But at the time I needed someone to be there and Barry was it. He told me I was beautiful, held me and brought me chocolate as a surprise. I needed what he offered.

We agreed from the start that it wouldn't be long-term. I certainly wasn't in love with him and called it off after a few weeks. Our parting was melodramatic with tears on both sides. I was addicted to the roller-coaster drama that had become a fixture in my life and his emotion-charged Italian-style was something that attracted me from the beginning. But I knew it was over.

Unfortunately, Barry didn't detach from my life easily and would contact me repeatedly over the following years. Every time I thought he'd finally got the message, he'd call again. Eventually I started screening his calls and stopped responding altogether.

Four years after we'd first met, Barry arrived unannounced on my doorstep. I didn't flatter myself that he was interested in

Lucretia Ackfield

my scintillating conversation. He'd dressed up for the occasion and looked good; trim, happy and very pleased to see me. He even knew exactly how long it had been since we'd last spoken.

He was also terribly charming. For him nothing had changed and if I'd crooked my little finger he would have been back in my bed. I didn't invite him in and could tell he was just as unavailable as ever. 'Have you married again?' he asked.

I couldn't believe his audacity. Did he honestly think that if I was married again I would 'entertain him' for a second?

'No, not yet,' I said politely. 'Maybe one day, but not yet.'

He asked about my travels and we talked about his work. He gave me his latest business card but I refused to give him my number. I told him our time together had been lovely but it was done. He seemed to accept my words and left shortly afterwards.

Two weeks later he was back on my doorstep and I couldn't believe it. Did he really think I would invite him back into my life and back into my bed? 'Barry,' I ground out between gritted teeth. 'I've tried to be

The Men I've Almost Dated

polite but you're just not getting it. What we had was lovely but it's over and you turning up here could be seen as stalking. So get off my porch right now and don't ever come back.'

I've never seen a man scurry before, but Barry definitely scurried. He scurried down my front stairs, across the lawn and into his car before driving off at a rapid pace.

I never heard from him again.

Lucretia Ackfield

'But You Were My Model For A Good Relationship!'

For better or worse, a wedding and marriage is bigger than two people. A separation and divorce is no different. I found myself confronted with my own pain and everyone else's feelings as well.

I relied on my friends a lot and most were incredibly patient. They listened to my confusion, my grief and observed my unpredictable behaviour as I swung from one extreme to the other, sometimes several times a day. It must have been exhausting for them. Most of them hung in there for me but some were unhappy about the choices I was making.

They thought things were great the way they were and didn't understand why I wanted to throw it all away. After all, while most of them had been single and navigating dating in their 20s I'd been in a nice secure relationship from the age of 18 with a man everyone loved.

The Men I've Almost Dated

The reactions were diverse.

The year before I left, Daniel and I bought a new car. Two weeks later I told Wanda I was thinking about leaving. 'You don't go out and buy a brand new car with someone and then leave them Lucretia!' she said scornfully. She was thoroughly fed up with me by that point and understandably our friendship didn't survive the separation.

When I did leave, my family was devastated. My parents lost a son and my sisters lost a brother. 'But you were my model for a good relationship!' wailed my sister Jasmine.

As if I didn't have enough pressure.

My parents kept inviting Daniel over for dinner for months after the break-up. He told me about the dinners and also told my parents they should be supporting me, not him. That's just what he was like. When I asked what was going on, Dad said angrily, 'It's none of your business if we invite Daniel over and we don't have to tell you about it!'

Dad was upset with me for rocking the boat and Mum also struggled with my choice. They would later tell friends what a

Lucretia Ackfield

'catch' Daniel was and how, less than a year after our separation, he'd been snapped up by someone else. When I asked Mum about those comments years later she said, 'We just thought you'd regret your decision.'

My parents loved me but, if I was looking for their approval, I was going in the wrong direction. I tried to understand where they were coming from but I didn't always feel very supported and their priorities seemed a little out of kilter.

Meanwhile, some female acquaintances acquired an air of smugness as they clung to their partners and hurried them out of my reach at social functions. Others who knew me as part of the Daniel/Lucretia partnership now felt a little awkward. They had known me as one part of a whole. Now I was just me.

Much of our society and culture is based on finding a mate and, if you're not seeing someone, people want you to find someone. I was asked a lot of questions and sometimes I didn't feel comfortable answering them. In hindsight I wish I'd had responses stockpiled for those awkward moments.

42

The Men I've Almost Dated

When yet another acquaintance or family member asked if I'd found a serious boyfriend yet, I could have said, 'No, I prefer having sex with lots of different people' or 'I've found several candidates, but I'm still deciding.'

If I was dating someone and was asked if it was getting serious, I could have said, 'No, we're still just practising. The sex needs a lot of work' or 'No, I thought I'd wait until he's finished university before we commit.'

Or, for the often-asked question of, 'Why can't you find someone to go out with?' I could have said, 'I'm holding out for a young Robert Redford' or 'I'm waiting until Justin Bieber becomes legal.'

If only I'd been quick-witted enough to say those things. Instead I laughed off most of the questions or simply changed the subject.

Two years into my newly single life, at an annual family gathering, I declared I wasn't really looking to get married again. My Dad's response was immediate. 'That's a real worry,' he said. 'You should be taking active steps to get married again.' His comment reflected the feelings of many others. I'd been safely packaged away in a relationship for a long time and they didn't have to worry about me. Now I was single, a curiosity, or perhaps a problem to be solved.

The same conversation included advice that it was just as well the latest man in my life had taken off because, being 26 (nine years my junior), he would have left me in the end anyway. Dad can be a little traditional in his views and a daughter who decided to leave her very worthy husband to be single in her thirties made him uncomfortable.

Nevertheless I could have done without that kind of feedback.

My sister Jasmine's comments that day were also pretty interesting. She told me I was weird because I didn't have an overwhelming desire to have children. Children weren't really on my radar at the time; I was still trying to work out how to be on my own and maybe find a new partner. 'You're very different from most women,' she said. It didn't feel like it was meant as a compliment. I guess you can always count on your family to be honest.

The Men I've Almost Dated

'Why are you still single?' became a common and somewhat maddening question over the ensuing months and years. People were incredulous that some man hadn't snapped me up. While this was flattering it was also awkward because I didn't have an answer. My fallback comment was simply, 'There's a lack of available talent out there'.

Uncle Donald suggested I hook up with one of the judges I was working with at the Law Courts. 'They'll have heaps of money,' he said.

'They're probably a little old for me.' I wasn't very enthusiastic about his suggestion. 'Besides, I'm quite happy to make my own money.'

My argument was dismissed out of hand.

'They'll just pop off and leave you with their money then,' he said. I think he was only half-joking. He then moved on to other matchmaking schemes. 'What about the other ones?' he asked. 'The ones who wear the gowns to work.'

'You mean the barristers?'

'Yeah, them. They'd have plenty of money.'

'Nope, I haven't found any that interest me and they're probably a little too conservative anyway,' I replied before excusing myself and heading rapidly towards the nearest bottle of alcohol.

Other well-meaning relatives would ask if I was really sure I'd made the right decision to leave. 'You don't regret it do you?' they'd ask anxiously.

'Of course not,' I'd respond. Then I'd amuse them with my latest dating disaster stories. It was a great way to divert attention.

I was volunteering as an English tutor with a recently-arrived refugee family from Sudan around the same time and even they had questions. I found myself talking to one of their friends about marriage and choices. Boris was a Sudanese, well-educated and married man in his mid-40s with five children.

'Why are so many Australians divorced and why don't their marriages last?' he asked. 'In our country people marry at 14 and remain together their entire lives.'

'Are they happy?' I asked.

'Yes,' he said. 'Why, in a country like Australia, where we have so many choices and education, do people make the wrong choices and marry the wrong people?'

His question was deceptively simple and not meant to cause offence. But it made me feel profoundly uncomfortable. There I was, a tertiary-educated, divorced woman in her mid-30s who in spite of all her knowledge, education and opportunities, had been unable to make her own marital relationship last.

I couldn't answer him.

Lucretia Ackfield

Relationship Amnesia

I gained a lot of new friends following my separation and divorce, but I lost a few old ones too. Some were so focused on who I used to be that they couldn't cope with my decision to leave Daniel. Others just didn't understand the new direction my life was taking.

A few were worn out because I felt the need to share everything I was going through. That's what extroverts do. We like to talk to others in order to work things out. It must have been exhausting for them.

My friends were used to the old me; the one in the stable long-term relationship with the nice partner. I was the friend they didn't have to worry about. The one who always had someone to spend the holidays with.

Many offered encouraging advice and shared their own dating disaster stories when I recounted my experiences. They were in relationships but could still remember what it was like to be 'out there'. They hadn't yet

The Men I've Almost Dated

succumbed to what I call 'relationship amnesia'. This happens when people in a relationship completely forget what it's like to be single and looking for love. People with this condition will make the following types of statements when you share your frustrations about trying to find Mr Right.

'You're too guarded.'

'You need to give them a chance.'

Then there's the comment that drives me absolutely crazy.

'Your expectations are too high.'

My friend Katie once shared this insight as she looked lovingly across the room at her partner Thomas. I'm pretty sure Katie hadn't settled for Mr Half-Way-to-What-I-Want when she moved in with him. He clearly met her expectations - whatever they were.

I didn't want to settle for something less than what I wanted. I was divorced once and 'settling' sounded like a recipe for another broken relationship.

My friend Jane said wanting to be attracted to someone from the start was shortsighted. 'Sometimes they grow on you when you get to know them,' she said. She implied my desire to feel fireworks, or at least a strong attraction, at the beginning of a relationship was unrealistic.

Meanwhile, my newly-engaged work colleague, Annie, questioned my preference for taller men. 'Maybe your expectations are too high and you should consider shorter men,' she said. 'Maybe you're being unrealistic.'

Her fiancé was taller than her.

Statistics showed it would be more difficult to find a partner as I got older so it seemed I should settle for what I could get. I know most of these comments were well-meaning, most of the time. My friends wanted me to be happy, like them. However, relationship amnesia meant they'd completely forgotten the expectations and standards they'd had while dating. They would shake their heads despairingly at the antics of friends like me while conveniently forgetting they used to do exactly the same things when they were single.

Unfortunately, I'd also acted under the influence of relationship amnesia.

My friend Wanda was single for most of my married life. She dated a few men but nothing ever worked out. She was a good-looking, intelligent and funny woman but just hadn't met the right one.

By our late twenties, Wanda was really disheartened by the whole dating scene. 'I just can't meet anyone,' she'd said despairingly as we sat at a local bar one night. 'There's just no one out there.'

It was at that moment, while ensconced in my safe long-term relationship, I offered my advice. 'You have to try Wanda,' I said helpfully. 'You have to flirt with them.'

'I do!' was her angry response as she stalked away.

It was probably one of the most insensitive things I've ever said. It was relationship amnesia at its worst and Wanda darling, if you're reading this, I'm really sorry.

Lucretia Ackfield

'Sisters Are Doing It For Themselves'

Being in a committed relationship means you usually consult your partner when making a major decision. Sometimes you even consult them regarding minor decisions. It's not about acquiescing to their every whim. It's more about compromise and trying to ensure you are both as happy as possible.

That's why, a year after my separation, I found myself standing cluelessly in a local furniture showroom. I'd left most of my furniture behind with Daniel and was decorating my new place from scratch. But all I could do was stand there in bewilderment looking at couch after couch. I couldn't even decide what colour I liked.

There I was a grown woman of 30-plus who made difficult decisions at work every day, negotiated with senior staff and used my initiative constantly. But I was filled with panic. What if I picked the wrong couch? What if I chose a style and a colour but, when I had it delivered, it looked like crap?

There was no one to ask and there would be no one to blame if it all went horribly wrong. I walked aimlessly around several stores that day with zero confidence in my ability to make a good choice. After 15 years with Daniel, I had lost my ability to choose furniture independently. It was kind of ridiculous really.

A few days passed before I finally gave myself a metaphorical slap and realised I could trust my own taste in couches. Besides, if it looked awful when I got it home I could send it back, throw a blanket over it, or list it on eBay.

I just wouldn't tell anyone about it.

Choosing furniture wasn't the only thing I had to do for myself. I now had to develop unique solutions to dilemmas I would have previously passed on as 'husband stuff'. It's amazing how creative you can become when there's no one around.

Lucretia Ackfield

'Sisters are doing it for themselves'[1] has become a personal theme song.

Sometimes I sing it through gritted teeth while attempting activities that really require two people, not just me. It's been the background music while I mutter, 'Get over you bastard' as I've flipped my queen size mattress, risking serious back injury and narrowly missing the light bulb. It's great for a weekly arm workout though.

I've also used the theme song for encouragement while trying to start the mower. Daniel did most of the mowing and maintenance when we were married but, as a single woman, I've been determined to do those things for myself.

That's why, two years into my single life (with my own lawn to maintain) you could have peered over my fence and found me pulling and tugging on the mower cord like a woman demented. Throughout the process I was vehemently hoping the neighbours weren't laughing hysterically as they

---

[1] *'Sisters are doing it for themselves'*: 1985 duet recorded by British pop duet Eurythmics and American soul singer Aretha Franklin.

watched me demonstrate yet another 'what not to do' exercise.

The mower would occasionally start but my triumph would be short-lived as it soon stalled in the dense scrub once known as my lawn. Then I'd have to start over.

Throughout this process my new housemate Sinesh loitered under the pergola with his mate Jimmy, watching as I became increasingly hot, sweaty and grass-covered. He seemed to find the sight of a grown woman swearing and fighting with a mower amusing.

I'd grown up in a blokey Australian culture where men helped women out with this sort of thing, so I expected more. I also thought a well-mannered man would have offered to help rather than laughing at me. But I was blinded by Sinesh's good looks. Next time I'll think more carefully before sleeping with a spoilt, good-looking man who shares my house, laughs at me while I work myself into a frenzy and doesn't offer to help. However, he did look hot wielding a vacuum (but I'll share more about that later).

Lucretia Ackfield

These days I pay my neighbour's son to mow the lawn. He's in early high school and definitely too young to be hot.

I've also been willing to attempt a range of handyman-type tasks while living alone (or with a useless male housemate). Paying someone to do the work for me is cost prohibitive and usually my pride prevents me asking for help. I'm the independent, feminist-type who wants to be as capable and self-sufficient as possible.

My newfound skills have led to some satisfying moments.

Not long after I moved into my house, Daniel dropped off some paperwork and I was able to intelligently ask his advice about the plumbing. There I was, a woman who could previously barely open a toolbox, expertly wielding an Allen key to remove a bath tap then discussing the 'seat' and its depth in the wall. The look on his face was priceless.

I didn't mention a male friend had shown me how to use the Allen key a few days earlier.

These days I also have my own toolbox overflowing with screws, hammers,

The Men I've Almost Dated

screwdrivers and miscellaneous other things previously known to me as 'man things' and a rechargeable drill of my own. In fact, I probably have more tools than most metrosexual men and I know how to use them baby!

There is however, a downside to my newfound confidence in attempting tasks previously relegated, in my mind, to the world of men. Men often seem to have the patience to fix things and put stuff together. Unfortunately, that patience escapes me.

I can do straightforward things. Putting together tables and my housemate's futon was a cinch. But the drawer in my china cabinet that's been jammed for the past 12 months still thwarts me. Every couple of months I'll jiggle it, wiggle it, stare at it and swear at it. Nothing works. After a few minutes my frustration takes over and I have to walk away. It's either that or throw a tantrum. One day I will finally slide that drawer effortlessly open and it will be like Christmas morning as I no longer remember what's in there.

I also improvise a lot. I may not be as efficient as someone who actually knows what they're doing, but I still get things done. My determination to be independent can take me down paths I think are quite ingenious and inventive. Other people just think I'm a little insane.

I confess there have been times when I've wished for a partner to share the load, like the day I found myself up a tree in a cemetery at 4.30am.

My dawn shenanigans were part of a bird rescue mission I'd begun about 11 hours earlier. I was up the tree carefully following the advice of a nice man called Reg, the wildlife rescue and animal ambulance man from the local council.

I'd found a baby bird on the footpath as I walked home the day before. It was clearly too young to be on its own and I couldn't leave it to its fate. I'm pretty sure its parents had tried to peck my eyes out that morning as I walked past on the way to the bus stop, so I didn't owe them any favours. Even so, I couldn't just walk away and leave the chick to become dinner for a local cat or dog.

I initially rang my friend Tara for some advice. She was at the pub - a sensible choice for a Friday night.

The Men I've Almost Dated

'Hi. Have you ever had to rescue a bird?' I asked.

'What?' she said.

'Have you ever had to rescue a bird?'

'What? A bird?' Tara asked again. She was wondering if I'd suffered a recent blow to the head.

'Yes. A bird. Have you ever had to rescue a bird?'

'Um…what are you talking about?'

I explained my predicament but Tara couldn't offer a solution. 'I don't know Lucretia. Maybe you just need to let nature take its course.'

She was in a pub eight kilometers away and I was standing beside a cemetery just before nightfall. There wasn't much she could do. I said my goodbyes and stood there staring at the bird for another minute or two before I turned and walked home. But I couldn't forget about it.

Twenty minutes later, in the dark, I was back at the cemetery armed with a shoebox and a mission. I was going to rescue that bird and return it at dawn.

Over the previous four years I'd walked the few blocks from my home to the cemetery for the ANZAC Day Dawn Service and had always been struck by the calmness of the graveyard. There was no fear, no ghosts, just peace.

Unfortunately, I didn't feel quite so brave standing beside the cemetery fence by myself, in the dark, at 4.30am. But I was committed to my task and, as the birds began twittering around me, I knew I had limited time before the chick's parents awoke properly and went into attack mode.

The chick had spent the night in my laundry (safely locked way from Super Puss, my cat, who clearly wanted a closer look at my temporary resident) and now chirped occasionally inside the shoebox on my front seat.

I flung myself over the five-foot cemetery fence, landed on my back, stood up, brushed myself off and opened my blue golf umbrella for protection against the chick's parents. I then collected my ice-cream bucket (filled with shredded newspaper) with strings attached (based on the advice of Ron – the wildlife rescue man I'd spoken to at the council the night before), and climbed the tree.

The Men I've Almost Dated

Have you ever tried to tie an ice-cream container to a branch, while balancing in the fork of a tree and hugging an IKEA umbrella in the crook of your neck? Let's just say it wasn't very relaxing. The strings kept sliding down the branch as I kept a wary eye on the parents. They were watching me closely but were either too sleepy to attack or simply trying to work out what the heck I was doing.

Most people were still in bed at dawn that Saturday. But a passing cyclist got a fright, developed the wobbles and nearly rode into the gutter when he spotted me. I guess it was pretty strange to see a woman up a tree, golf umbrella held aloft, in a cemetery at dawn.

Another man jogged by shortly afterwards but he determinedly pretended I wasn't there. This confirmed my frequent lament that chivalry was dead. He could have offered to help me but instead he just jogged out of sight.

Once the ice-cream container was in place, I returned to my car for the baby bird. There was no way it would survive being flung over the fence so this time I would have to take the long way around. I donned my gardening gloves (freshly purchased the night before to protect my hands from baby bird peckings), picked up the shoebox, grabbed my umbrella and walked the half block around the corner to the graveyard entrance.

I was feeling a little anxious when I reached the tree. I'd had some earlier fears of being attacked by an opportunistic rapist or murderer in the dim pre-dawn light. Now I feared I might lose an eye or ear lobe through a bird mauling.

Climbing the tree while grasping the umbrella and shoebox, was a challenge. The parent birds watched me carefully but everything was going according to plan.

Then it all went to hell.

Hugging the branch, holding the umbrella and opening a shoebox at the same time proved a little more complicated than my early morning brain could handle.

Once the lid came off the box, the baby bird started to cheep and its parents started to squawk. I started to panic as I chased the bird around the box with one hand. The parents started dive-bombing and I panicked even more.

The Men I've Almost Dated

Somehow I grabbed the bird (gardening gloves are not great for dexterity – lesson learned) and flung it into the ice-cream container.

Both the box and I fell out of the tree. I took off, running through the gravestones, waving the umbrella wildly above my head pursued, in my mind at least, by a horde of angry birds. There might have been a whole flock back there but I wasn't pausing to find out.

By the time I got back to my car, the baby bird had already hopped out of the makeshift nest I'd so carefully created for its comfort and was sitting on the branch with its parents nearby. I guess that's gratitude for you.

I headed home but the shoebox stayed where it was. The birds were welcome to it.

Super Puss was waiting at the front door and his expression indicated he thought I'd lost my mind. Maybe he was right.

The whole thing would have been much easier if I'd had a man with me – at least he could have run interference during the bird attack.

Market Competition

While I've developed a great capacity for solving dilemmas around the home, I've found many parties and social occasions more difficult to navigate. They can be full of landmines when you're single, particularly when most people are in couples.

These events shouldn't be daunting but most of us have watched Bridget Jones's escapades. We know about the questions friends and strangers ask 30-somethings about having children and the absence of a life partner.

However there is something far worse than commenting on a woman's lack of children as she watches her years of fertility gallop off over the horizon and out of sight.

I call it 'market competition' and it's not well-meaning.

Market competition is about women competing for resources - men. It's about watching your man like a hawk and keeping all other women, especially single women, away from him. Women do this really well and it can happen in any social situation, on the street, in the office or at parties. Women demonstrate the behaviour subtly or obviously and it happens a lot.

Kay was an example of market competition at its finest. She was the wife of a colleague and we met at work functions. It didn't matter how many times I tried to engage her in polite, friendly conversation, she would utter only the shortest responses and occasionally shoot me a steely 'fuck off' gaze. Kay wasn't excessively introverted and interacted with everyone else in a positive way. I wracked my brains but I couldn't think of anything I might have done to upset her. I'd only met her twice before and was always polite.

Then my friend and colleague, Jemma, shed some light on the real issue. Kay had treated her exactly the same way until Jemma got a boyfriend. Almost overnight, Kay became friendly and normal because Jemma was off the market.

Kay's husband was not the type to stray. He adored his wife and showed it. But I'd seen her physically pull him in the opposite direction when she spotted me nearby. In her eyes I was competition and we would never be friendly while I was single. She was attached and I was not. This made me a threat, apparently.

Kay was an extreme case because she was so obviously rude. But her behaviour wasn't unusual. Many attached women just don't like single women around their menfolk.

There are some single women who habitually pursue men who already have partners. They will be open to the advances of attached men and act in a predatory way. But if you're at a party, and your partner is committed, it's unlikely another woman will threaten your relationship.

So either most women feel insecure in their relationships – what a depressing thought - or rational thought processes vanish at events like my friend Rhonda's birthday party.

My outfit was pretty conservative - no cleavage and a skirt down to my knees. It certainly didn't scream, 'I'm a slut who is up for absolutely anything and I'm here to steal your man.'

I arrived around 8pm and looked forward to chatting to some people I knew and perhaps meeting some new ones. But it didn't work out that way. Although the birthday girl and her family made me very welcome, not many others did. The acquaintances I knew only stopped for a brief hello before hiding themselves away in a corner. This left me hanging around the kitchen, smiling hopefully at passersby and pretending I was comfortable. All I really wanted to do was disappear.

Some people smiled as they walked by and most women took careful note of my outfit using that rude once-over glance women often give to each other: that horrible way women check each other out when you start at the top of the head, move your eyes down to the toes, then sweep your way back up to the head again. Whenever this happens I always wonder if I should hike up my skirt, give a cheeky smile and ask 'Do you see something you like?' At least it might shock them into better behaviour.

Lucretia Ackfield

If I did talk to a man, his girlfriend or wife would swiftly move in and move him on.

I spent a lot of time staring intently at the bookshelves and loitering by the drinks table that night. Observers probably assumed I was a far-sighted, book-obsessed alcoholic.

The whole situation was very familiar and I left less than two hours after I arrived.

It was an example of how some people just don't know what to do around single women. Single men don't appear to have this problem. I'm not sure why this is but it feels a little unfair.

When you're single, some men will check you out when their girlfriend or wife isn't looking. But a decent normal male who tries to make you feel welcome will often find his girlfriend or wife soon hanging onto his arm with a determined 'he's mine' stronghold. Or, if she's across the room, he'll receive furious glances and a few sharp words in the car on the way home.

I sometimes wonder if people remember what it was like to be single in a room full of couples. I'm a confident person but after Rhonda's party I felt pretty awful. I can only imagine how shy women feel in the same situation. Then again, perhaps they have abandoned parties altogether and choose to be hermits, spending their evenings online shopping, consuming ice-cream and watching chick flicks.

I have wondered if there's something wrong with me. Do people dislike me on sight? Even when I've laughed their behaviour off, underneath it still hurts. Most of the time these women had never met me but it seemed their minds were already made up about who I am.

In my bitchier moments I've felt like saying (when yet another woman has dragged her male partner away) 'Honey, I'm really not interested in your pudgy-around-the-middle, boyfriend/husband in the bad tie who has taken over your study with his Dungeons and Dragons collection, hogs the bed and whose mother is a bat straight from hell who rearranges your cupboards.'

So far I've managed to resist this temptation.

I have developed a few strategies to help me navigate these challenging social situations. I try to arrive in the first hour so I

can meet people when they first enter the
room and before the cliques form. You'll
also find me volunteering to help with the
food as the host or hostess is always grateful
and it gives me an excuse to chat to people
as I circulate with the trays.

People are more likely to engage with
someone who looks friendly so I always
wear my best smile. No one wants to talk
to a grouch. I also politely discourage any
men who become too friendly if they've
arrived with a woman or they're wearing a
wedding ring.

My final strategy often involves leaving
early. If I think the party will be a single
girl's night from hell I'll tell the hosts I have
to leave early for some reason. For example,
I might have an early start in the morning,
another party to go to, another friend's
birthday to celebrate or a family
commitment. It's a little white lie but is
often the only way to keep my sanity and
self-esteem intact.

If you try these strategies and still find
yourself circling the food table or perusing
the artwork with intense concentration you
could, as I'm often tempted to do, stand up,

The Men I've Almost Dated

pull your shirt over your head and run around the room yelling, 'I'm here and I'm single and I'm not going away you motherfuckers!!!'

At least they won't be able to ignore that.

Single women aren't always treated badly by other women, We can be just as cruel to ourselves. I'm guilty of this too because I've caught myself doing the unthinkable – comparing myself to other women.

I usually like myself, just the way I am. But there have been times when my self-confidence has taken a short holiday. On one occasion, I found myself walking through a shopping centre and comparing myself to other women. I call these competitor days; I was in competition with every other woman and beside each of them I found myself wanting.

Every one of them was more attractive than me. They were alone or with partners, dressed fashionably and looking beautiful. I, on the other hand, was alone and unappealing.

I found myself thinking, 'Why don't I look as good as them? Why doesn't a guy that good looking want to go out with me?

Lucretia Ackfield

Why did I wear this outfit today? I'm so boring. Why do I even bother anyway? Look at all these beautiful women and so many of them are so young - what happened to my youth? Why would any man look at me when I'm in my mid/late thirties and working on body 'maintenance' while there's beautiful 20-somethings available?'

I even found myself giving women the once-over. That's when I knew I was in trouble because I hate the once-over! But on that day, I found myself doing it to other women. It was awful, ridiculous and demeaning and I cringe when I think about it. Comparing myself to others is a complete waste of time.

There will always be another woman who is more glamorous, thinner, curvaceous, smarter or more 'everything' than me. I could spend a lifetime comparing myself to others and coming up short. But instead I remind myself that I will never win that competition. The only thing I'll do is make myself feel bad.

I usually prefer to spend my time building others up rather than tearing them down, stiletto by stiletto. But not all women feel the same.

I was out with my girlfriend Carrie one night when she pointed to a young girl standing nearby and said, 'I love seeing girls like that when I go out because it makes me feel so much better about myself.'

The girl was in her early 20s, a little on the plump side and was wearing a short skirt and a low cut top that was two sizes too small. She was having fun with her friends and obviously felt good about what she was wearing. But Carrie focused on the girl's perceived flaws to feel better about herself.

I wish I could say this was an aberration but I've heard a lot of bitchy comments made about the dress sense, size and hairstyle of women over the years. It happened again recently when I was out with two friends on a Friday night. A young woman in her late teens passed us in a club and men turned to watch her walk across the room. She was young, with a sky-high skirt and breasts out for the world to see. She was displaying her body without shame and, although she looked like she might topple over at any moment due to her amazingly high heels, I thought she looked fabulous.

My two friends were vicious in their comments about her appearance. 'Who does she think is? She's a bit obvious isn't she,' they said. They despised this woman because they were envious of attributes they believed she had, but they lacked.

I couldn't join in and even now I don't really understand why women behave this way.

The young girl was young, beautiful and confident enough to put on an outfit she liked and was having fun with her friends. It seemed that was enough to make her a target for competitiveness. I know I've occasionally wondered aloud if people have looked in a mirror to make sure an outfit suits their body shape before they leave the house. But the level of vitriol some women direct at each other when they simply look good or are attracting attention is just embarrassing and demeaning.

Shouldn't we be supporting our sisters instead of tearing them down?

Cyberstalking and Fairytales

If you're single, female and in your 30s you've probably come home late one Saturday night after a few drinks and sent a Facebook friend request to someone you've got a crush on. Or you've put his name into Google and scrolled through the search results.

Before the online era we asked friends, family and colleagues about potential love interests. But today, with so much technology at our fingertips, our access to information is almost limitless. A Google search can identify a man's family members, his blog or fundraising activities. Then you can move on to LinkedIn and discover his work history and industry contacts. After this you can open Facebook, view his photos and sometimes read his wall conversation with his friends.

Facebook photos can reveal a lot about a man and then you can creatively fill in the gaps. Happy family photos at weddings and Christmas – he loves his family; photos doing extreme sports - he's an adrenalin junkie; photos in other countries – he likes to travel; photos of him at every social event with a bottle of Jim Beam in his hand – he's an alcoholic. You can make so many assumptions based on the barest of details.

It may seem a little intrusive, voyeuristic even, to research someone without their knowledge but people know most of their online information is public. I also know men do their share of cyberstalking too.

One of my blind dates, James, almost cancelled on me because of my Facebook profile picture – I was proudly holding my day-old nephew. He immediately rang our mutual friend and asked anxiously, 'Are you setting me up with some woman who's just given birth?'

We laughed about it later but, as a woman trying to attract a single man, I should have considered how my online information might attract or repulse a potential suitor.

The Men I've Almost Dated

I often cyberstalk people I'm curious about but cruising other people's Facebook pages can leave you feeling lousy.

I accepted a Facebook request from a new friend late one Saturday night and as I perused her wall and friends I saw a photo of Peter. He was a hot guy who'd been around the edges of my social scene for months. He flirted a lot but always seemed just out of my reach. But now I could see his Facebook page and couldn't resist taking a look at his photos. Then I saw images of him and his beautiful girlfriend and suddenly my world seemed a little less shiny. They looked so happy together and she was young and beautiful.

Peter had spent the last few months coming on to me but he was in a relationship with someone else. There it was in digital colour; photos of him with his girlfriend at a wedding just weeks earlier.

I felt stupid and naïve. My hopes for a fairytale ending were dashed.

I used to wonder if my fruitless search for the perfect life partner was the result of too many fairytales as a child. Snow White received the elixir of life from her prince,

Lucretia Ackfield

Rapunzel was saved from the tower by a man climbing her long plaited hair, and there are so many other examples where women were saved from a bad situation by a man.

But over the years I've had to let go of the idea of being rescued. I have to rescue me and then, if I'm lucky, I'll find a good man who doesn't need rescuing and he'll walk beside me and share my life. I guess I've realised fairytales are just that, fairy tales. Stories told by or about little winged females with no visible fat cells and glamorous, skimpy costumes.

With no partner prospects on the horizon, I've also contemplated what life might be like as a single old woman. I've wondered if the 70-year-old woman I once saw at the shops could be me one day. She was dressed in a bright floral dress, blocking the aisle with her shopping trolley and struggling with a cane.

It wasn't exactly an uplifting thought. But there might be no one, and definitely no man, to take care of me when I'm old. Instead there'll be a few kindly relatives to look out for their dear old auntie. They'll

The Men I've Almost Dated

take me shopping once a week and follow me slowly around the supermarket as I hover indecisively between two brands of beans. Perhaps there will also be invitations to major family events where I'll constantly yell, 'What?' when my hearing aid is on the blink.

In these darker moments I believe 'the one' may never come. It doesn't matter how often I read my horoscopes, visit psychics or ask the Universe for a sign that 'the one' is near. I might always be single.

However, being the eternal optimist, I always regroup and think what if there is someone great just around the corner? It would be churlish to give up hope a altogether. That's when I sneak a peak at my latest horoscopes or make an appointment with the psychic my best friend visited last week.

Maybe he could be just around the corner and I need to be prepared for it. Knowing it could be on the cards (literally) gives me something great to look forward to…let's just call it planning for the future.

Lucretia Ackfield

It's the eternal contradiction of the single life, to swing from hope to despair about men, often within minutes.

There have also been many times when I've emerged fresh from another break-up and become addicted to seeking answers for my rather pathetic love life from the horoscopes. Whether I'm online or have picked up the latest trashy fashion magazine in the checkout line, my horoscope is the first thing I look for.

Does the Universe have a wonderfully fabulous gift-wrapped package waiting for me later today, this week or this month? The answer will be there, I'm sure of it.

Horoscopes are like the spiritual chiropractor for the single girl. They help us redirect our energies and crack our splintered spirits back into shape.

Sometimes they are also terribly misleading and we'll misinterpret them as we seek answers that validate our deepest desires and dreams. Yes, he will come back and it will be wonderful. Yes, that hot guy will ask me out.

When the messages are less uplifting like 'there are challenges ahead' or 'change is

The Men I've Almost Dated

coming' we convince ourselves those challenges and changes will only be positive. Or, if we are feeling really low, the horoscope will simply confirm the belief that our lives are truly in the toilet.

I'll also read the horoscopes of my lover or potential lover to gain insights about his character and how his life might relate to mine. Perhaps his horoscope might give me some guidance on how to approach him and persuade him to fall in love with me immediately.

I'm aware this approach is a little flawed and some horoscopes are not 100 percent reliable. There are some very inauthentic sources out there.

One of my former work colleagues, Jackson, once shared his fond memories of working at a local newspaper in his younger days. Apparently he and his mates earned a few extra dollars composing horoscopes. Unfortunately, none of them were psychic.

So perhaps when it comes to the horoscopes we should take my friend Cassie's approach. At the end of each year she buys all the trashy magazines she can find and seeks answers from within their horoscope pages. If the predictions for the year ahead are negative or don't meet her expectations, she throws them out.

But she always keeps the good ones.

The Men I've Almost Dated

PART 2
Dysfunctional Dating and Other Disasters

Lucretia Ackfield

The Categories of Man

When I became single at 32, I didn't have a clue about the miscommunication, illusions and downright deception that existed in the gaping chasm between men and women. Instead I began my journey full of wonder and naiveté, a bit like Alice in Wonderland. I was curious about the whole 'man thing' so I metaphorically stuck my head somewhere I shouldn't and fell down a rabbit hole where I met lots of weird creatures. Except in my life, the weird creatures were men.

I can't say my experiences have always been positive but they certainly have been eye-opening. Due to my general cluelessness and yes, sometimes self-destructive romantic optimism, I've also pursued the wrong men. Repeatedly. Frustration and heartbreak have been regular visitors in my home.

These days I hope I'm more skilled at identifying the ones I shouldn't invest

emotional energy in. I've also come up with
some categories to help me do this. My
challenge is to identify these men early so
I can extract myself quickly and move on
to a better and hopefully more functional
human being.

Here are just some of the Categories of
Man I've stumbled into in my 30s.

Mr No-Show

A Mr No-Show is very disappointing.
You'll believe he has potential and he'll be
attentive, pursue you, ask for your number
and arrange a date shortly afterwards.

Then he'll pull out of your date with no
explanation or some lame excuse. One
simply messaged his cancellation with a,
'You seem like the nicest girl, but I don't
think I'm the right kind of man for you.'

What, the kind of man who shows up?

When I walked into a nightclub with my
friend Jennifer, I didn't know I would soon
be introduced to one of the silliest Mr No-
Shows I have ever had the misfortune to
meet. It was mid-week and Jennifer had
convinced me to attend a singles-event. Just
the idea created discomfort and
awkwardness within me but, as we entered

the room, I was mentally geared to keep an open mind.

The event involved placing a group of single men and women of similar ages in a room and giving them free drinks. Everyone was going to mingle and perhaps meet the love of their life or at least their next coffee date. We found ourselves chatting to a man called Jeff and his friends. They were all well dressed, articulate and relaxed. I found myself drawn to Jeff and when he asked for my number I said, 'Yeah, sure'.

I scrabbled through my purse for a few seconds looking for a pen and paper before realising he'd whipped out his mobile phone and was waiting patiently to type in my details. Most of my dating had occurred in the eighties so I was a bit behind the times.

Jeff messaged later that night saying how great it had been to meet me. Our flirtation continued by text and two days later, he asked me out. Everything was going well. His messages were attentive, complimentary and lightly flirtatious. He even suggested a great venue for our date on Saturday night. But on Thursday, when I asked what time

we should meet, I received no response.
Instead I was greeted with…nothing.

I was confused. Why go to the effort of
setting up a day and venue if he didn't want
to meet me? Two weeks later, while out
with some similarly inebriated girlfriends,
I decided to get to the bottom of the Mr No-
Show mystery. My polite text read as
follows:

*ME: Um, just wondering if everything's
okay with you and what happened to our
date?*

*JEFF: Sorry bout our date. Had a few
serious dramas with my mother in hospital.
Just been stressed out due to my mother's
cancer situation. Hopefully, we can catch up
this weekend. Only if you're free. J*

Jeff had mentioned that his mother was
undergoing cancer treatment so I believed
his explanation. After all, I'm not a bitch.

We exchanged a few more messages and
he asked what I did for work. When I
mentioned I was writing a book about being
single he asked questions about that too.
Then he suggested we catch up that
weekend but when I mentioned the times I
was free, he seemed to lose interest. My

plans did include another singles event with Jennifer but, as Jeff hadn't actually met me for a date yet, I didn't think it was a big deal and I told him about it. I explained it was basically research for my book and I'd be my friend's wingman. His response came a day later.

JEFF: As for weekend. Seems like you have a lot of options plus work. Maybe catch up next weekend. I might stay in and visit my mum. Hope you have a good time at that singles night.

This guy was just messing me around. My next message illustrated my frustration.

ME: I'm not sure why you keep asking me out but not following through. I was hoping you were different to the other men in my book.

JEFF: Thank you for your honesty. I did have my reservations on my thoughts about you when we meet. It just confirms what I was feeling. I'm assuming you wanted to go out with me for your book due to the fact you highlighted me to a couple of chapters in your book. I understand. I thought you be actually interest in me that night. But I knew it couldn't be true. I'm not that lucky.[sic]

Lucretia Ackfield

He had completely misunderstood me.

ME: Hey settle down. I did want to go out with you. The only ones who usually go in my book are the ones who behave badly. I wouldn't have said yes if I didn't want to see you.

JEFF: My apologies, I just found you very gorgeous and didn't understand why you were talking to me. Sorry for taking things out of context. Hope you can forgive me. Seeing you have a full on weekend. Are you still interested ion meeting up next weekend?

ME: Sure, as long as you don't wig out again.

ME: Promise not to wig again. Well your working Sat and I'm assuming you have your singles night with the girls Sun. So it seems your weekend is full. Next week's sounds good. Hopefully you don't have a busy one next weekend [sic]

ME: No worries, I'm sure I can find other things to do to amuse myself this weekend.

JEFF: Got me thinking what things you could do to amuse yourself. Or am I thinking to much again bout your text message =)

The Men I've Almost Dated

Seriously. What the fuck? This guy had stood me up once, flipped out over nothing, had made no confirmed plans to see me and was now making suggestive comments. And yes, his text spelling was really that bad. It was time to pull the plug. I didn't message Jeff again and he never followed up.

When I recounted the episode to Mum she asked, 'Did it ever occur to you that he was all just bullshit from the start?' 'Yes,' I confessed. 'I just wanted to see how far he'd take it.'

The Perpetual Flirt

A Perpetual Flirt will never take his hints and compliments any further. He'll touch you on the arm, hold eye contact, seek you out and make you laugh every time he sees you. But if he's had several chances to ask you out and he hasn't, then he won't. He may be a ladies man or just have commitment issues. Whatever the reason, he will never take it to the next level.

Dion flirted persistently with me for a couple of months and all the signs were there. But when I eventually tried to give the situation a gentle nudge by asking him out, he told me he'd never been interested in dating me. My brain whirred in confusion and for a moment I wondered if I'd misread the signals. But I knew it wasn't all in my head and he'd definitely been coming on to me, even if he denied it.

Like all Perpetual Flirts, Dion didn't exhibit stellar social behaviour. He just thought he could get away with it. And for the record, if you think a guy is flirting with you, he probably is. But sometimes he'll be too chicken to admit it.

The Newly Single Man

Some people say the best way to get over a relationship is to 'get back on the horse'. Often (for men) this basically means getting onto, or literally into, someone else. The Newly Single Man, also known as Mr Just-Out-Of-A-Relationship or Mr I'm-Not-Over-Her-Yet, seems to follow this ethos more than women. Unfortunately, the women they get 'into' are often left behind rather rapidly.

You can be attracted to a Newly Single Man because he's sad, depressed and just a little tragic. You'll want to take care of him or help him get over it. You may even think you could be the 'real one' they are meant to be with.

Unfortunately, these men are in mourning and more often than not you'll be the transitional woman. You might have a laugh together and you'll help him to heal but then he'll discover his heart is mended and will gallop off with someone else.

I've been with men who are so obviously not over their last partner that they can't get it up in the bedroom. In these situations you can of course stick at it until it sticks back up again but it's probably wiser to hightail it out the door. If his penis isn't ready for another woman then his heart sure as hell isn't either.

The Newly Single Man needs to remember who he is again. The longer he and his ex were together, the longer he will usually need to get his head and heart straight again. You can wait around if you want, but you'll risk heartbreak and missing out on a man who is emotionally available, right now.

Besides who wants to nurse a man back to emotional health and a possible erection when you could be out now having fun with a man who's in good working order.

The Old Dog

The Old Dog has journeyed many emotional kilometres in his 40-plus life. He's the veteran of a long-term relationship and may have shared custody of his children.

He's cocky, fit and has a series of emotional walls that it will take a pretty special woman to climb or pull down.

He'll appreciate a good-looking woman and will love to verbally spar with someone who can keep up. He'll probably sleep with you too. But don't get too attached. This man is so battle-scarred, usually by the woman who left, that he's unlikely to let you get close anytime soon.

You'll have to work really hard because he'll like flitting around the edges of a real relationship. But at the first sign of any real intimacy, the Old Dog will be looking for the nearest escape route.

This world-weary man has been though a lot and is not ready to let go of the past so he can move into the future with you. Put simply, he's a survivor who will run alone

94

for a long time; a bit like an old stray dog who's been beaten too many times and is unable to trust a human again.

The Serial Texter

When you first meet the Serial Texter you'll have things in common, share some laughs, the attraction will be mutual and he'll ask for your number. But it won't go anywhere and all you'll gain is an inflated phone bill and a deflated ego.

The Serial Texter will send you a text message soon after you meet. His following messages will be amusing, flirty and frequent. He won't ask you out and there will be limited, if any, actual phone conversations. But there will be lots and lots of text messages.

He'll ask what you're up to and where you're going with your friends. He'll seem genuinely interested in your life. But he won't ask to see you in person to discuss it.

If you decide to be a little more obvious and start sex-ting, he'll definitely be interested in that. And if you invite him over for sex then he may even show up. But, you still won't get a date and to be honest, sometimes the sex won't be great either.

Lucretia Ackfield

You'll persevere and he'll be charming and witty. If you call, he'll call you back because he's polite and he does like you. But the Serial Texter won't initiate a verbal conversation and he won't ask you out on a date. This situation can go on for weeks or months if you let it.

I reconnected with Harry the Serial Texter at a party held by a mutual friend. We hadn't talked for years but soon relaxed in each other's company. He asked for my number and began messaging me soon afterwards. He was always checking in to see what I was doing and was very flirtatious. But it was all via text message.

Harry had recently emerged from a long-term relationship so I figured he needed some time before committing to a date. Over the next three weeks I kept responding to his messages with the expectation that he would eventually ask me out.

But he just sent messages. Lots and lots of messages.

We did graduate to the occasional phone call, always initiated by me, but as the weeks rolled on Harry gave no sign that he wanted to see me in person.

The Men I've Almost Dated

In my naiveté (and because he was hot), I allowed the texting to escalate to sex-ting. It was fun and I invited him over a couple of times. He visited, never stayed and kept messaging. But he still didn't ask me out and as time passed I knew he was never going to.

Eventually I asked him to stop contacting me. It was one of the few occasions when I knew I was getting emotionally involved but it wasn't going anywhere. It was time for some self-preservation.

'You have to stop communicating with me,' I said. 'I can't do this anymore. I want more than you can give me right now.'

'Can't I even talk to you at all?' he pleaded.

'No,' I said. 'It's just too hard for me.'

Then I disconnected, flung the phone across my room and indulged in a bout of frustrated tears. I knew it was the right thing to do. Harry couldn't offer anything more than text messages and a mounting phone bill. But I was still disappointed.

Lucretia Ackfield

The Single-Attached Man

Single-Attached Man will be cunningly disguised as a nice guy and you will share lots of eye contact, smiles and chemistry. You'll see him socially and the pattern will continue. You'll feel quite attached to him and will enjoy the way he seeks you out for a chat and some special attention. This can go on for weeks or months.

Then you'll discover, often through social media (the friend and foe of every single woman), that he has a partner and your world will crumble around the edges a little. What the hell was he playing at and why didn't he mention his partner?

The answer is simple; he's a Single-Attached Man.

Some of these men won't progress to cheating. But they will confuse women by acting single, available and interested until the truth comes out.

Of course, you can dispel all the confusion by having an early and honest conversation involving the very pertinent question, 'Are you single or do you have a girlfriend or wife?' But sometimes we avoid asking this question because we want to believe we have found a decent man and we don't want to consider the alternative. Could we be our own worst enemy in this scenario?

The Taken Man

The Taken Man will be married or in a relationship with someone else when he makes a pass at you. You will know he's already in a relationship when this happens.

Sometimes it can be easy to fall into, or seriously consider, a relationship with a Taken Man. You may even allow yourself a brief daydream about a time when he dumps his current partner to be with you. Occasionally this will happen. But it's usually in the movies.

Men who have wives or girlfriends and then make a pass at you are not usually great long-term options. Even if a Taken Man did leave his wife for me, I'd always worry he might repeat the performance and trade me in a few years later.

However, I am frequently surprised at the transparency of their lies. A Taken Man can tell you with a straight face that his partner doesn't want to have sex anymore or he can't leave because she's emotionally

unstable. One delightful man told my friend
Carrie that he'd separated from his wife but
they were still sharing a house for the sake
of their children. Carrie wanted to believe
him but in the end it was all lies. His wife
had no idea what he was up to.

A Taken Man is in his current
relationship because he wants to be there.
His life is his own and so are his choices.
He's just hitting on you because you look
good and he doesn't want to change his
cushy home situation while he plays
the field.

When a Taken Man comes onto me
(often while his partner is nearby) I've often
thought 'Why is he doing this? Doesn't he
care about his wife?' and 'Is he just stuck in
a bad relationship?'

None of these thoughts are helpful
because yes, he could be a genuinely good
person who is stuck in a difficult situation.
Or he could just be another immature boy
trying to force both his hands into the
lolly jar.

The Men I've Almost Dated

The Controlling Snake

Most men I've met haven't been deliberately malicious. They've just had issues and I've been collateral damage.

Unfortunately, others aren't as benign. A Controlling Snake, for example, will insidiously slip into your life and slowly squeeze the very essence out of you. He will seem perfectly charming on the surface but the red flags will soon start to appear. I've been lucky enough to avoid these men. The Universe has kindly steered them out of my path. But some friends haven't been quite so lucky.

Marina had been dating Dirk for a couple of months when she told me, 'I used to think he was too controlling. But now I know he just cares about me a lot.'

I tried to query this comment but Marina had already dismissed the red flag she'd planted in front of me. A few months later, as I left her house after a mid-week takeaway dinner, Marina asked me to take the pizza boxes home with me. If Dirk found out I'd visited then he'd want to know every single detail of what was discussed and Marina just couldn't face the grilling. A few years have now passed and Marina and Dirk are still together. But her confidence and self-esteem are almost non-existent. He always wants to know where she is, who she is talking to and what she's doing. He is controlling and has suffocated her sense of self.

It's been disturbing to watch.

I've known other successful and independent women who've become under-confident, self-doubting and self-loathing shadows of their former selves because of a Controlling Snake. One friend would message me from a cupboard while her partner went on a violent rampage throughout the house. But she'd always beg me not to call the police or come over. In her work life she could take on the world and achieve amazing things. But at home her life was completely controlled by someone else.

I've managed to identify some key warning signs to help identify these men early. A Controlling Snake won't display all these traits simultaneously but he may just let one or two slip out while he keeps you in line. This is a good checklist if you're starting to doubt your own judgement. If any of the following sounds familiar in your relationship then you may want to consider your options…then run like hell!

1. Your friends are concerned about the way he treats you. If your friends don't like him it's probably worth investigating why.
2. When you go out alone, he will constantly contact you by phone or text message to ask what you're doing. He'll disguise his motives with lines like, 'I miss you so much when we're apart' or 'I just want to know that you're safe'. You'll begin thinking that receiving five messages during your girls' night out is normal.
3. He doesn't encourage any social pursuits or interests that don't include him.
4. He is not supportive of your dreams or ambitions and will frequently say they aren't realistic or achievable.
5. He eavesdrops on your conversations, asks to see your phone bills and then

interrogates you about who you speak to when he's not around.

6. He tells you that you cannot speak to some of your friends and makes you tell them this by text while he watches.

7. He controls all the money coming into your household.

8. He pressures you to dress the way he likes, denigrates your dress style or suggests that you're dressing in a deliberately provocative way to seduce other men. If he disapproves of an outfit you're wearing, you will change because it will be easier than listening to his niggling comments all night.

9. He doesn't like entertaining and it's sometimes easier to ask your friends to take their wine bottles home with them when they leave. Answering questions about who was over and what you did will be an excruciating experience best avoided.

10. When you fight and he gets angry, you get scared.

11. He discourages most of your friendships and your social circle is reduced to people he believes are appropriate.

The Men I've Almost Dated

12. He's jealous of your family.
13. He criticises who you are, what you
    think and what you believe in.
14. He is verbally, physically or
    emotionally abusive.

Also know that Controlling Snakes can
frequently charm others because they will be
great at wearing that 'social mask'. But
don't believe him when he says you're the
one with the problem; just get out.

The Hors De Oeuvres Man

My friend Dianne once shared a story
about Mick, a man she was 'kind of' seeing.

Dianne was a successful, professional
woman in her thirties who'd dated Mick two
years earlier before he'd broken it off so he
could date someone else (first warning
sign!). Now Mick was once again floating
around the edges of Dianne's world.
He always paid her just enough attention to
keep her interested but he was never really
available. Mick would make contact and be
around for a week or so, then disappear for a
few weeks before popping up again.

'I like him,' Dianne told me. She hoped
for something more from this man;

something more serious. 'The way he keeps coming back is a good sign, I think,' she said. But Mick kept repeating the same old pattern over and over again and Dianne began to wonder if it would ever grow into something more substantial.

Unfortunately, she'd become entangled with an Hors De Oeuvres Man. Mick was like the pig-in-a-blanket or chicken wing you take from a cocktail tray before dinner. He would offer Dianne just a small taste and then be gone. Unfortunately, he was never going to commit to something more - he was never going to be a banquet.

The Younger Man

Younger men are everywhere when you're single, in your thirties and just out of a relationship. You will be at bars, clubs or restaurants minding your own business and suddenly a Younger Man will be standing in front of you or checking you out from the other side of the room. They will be almost fearless.

I once walked past a young 20-something sitting at a bar. He touched my arm and when I looked back he simply raised an eyebrow and jerked his head back a little as if to say, 'What do you reckon?' Needless to say, I kept walking. I require a little more effort than that!

Some younger men will want to date you while others will only want to fuck you. They will all be very direct and it can be liberating and exhilarating.

But it's not about being a 'cougar' (I seriously loathe that term!). Women are not generally stalking young men like they are antelopes and we're wild animals of prey. They find us. And when they do, it can be a lot of fun.

But there are some things to remember when you become entangled with these youngsters. Firstly, remember large age-gaps can lead to short relationships. There are some exceptions but, if you tend to get a little too attached too quickly, just protect your heart and be careful.

You also need to be prepared for some censorious looks from strangers if you're dating a Younger Man. I've found it interesting that men are often more accepting and understanding of this type of relationship. Perhaps it's because of the whole Mrs Robinson fantasy? Women may not be quite as gracious – they'll be worried about someone like you sleeping with their sons in a few years time.

Your friends will probably encourage you to do whatever feels right. Take this advice and don't feel guilty. It's your life and this is your time.

And lastly, there's the sex.

Women reach their sexual peak as they approach 40. Men reach it at 18. This adds up to a lot of fun in the older woman-younger man relationship.

They can often go longer and more often in the bedroom. And because you're older and more confident than when you were in your 20s, you'll probably be more comfortable telling them what you want. They will be eager to learn. And of course, your experience will have taught you a few tricks of your own to please him too. The only problem may be finding a reason to keep your clothes on.

At one point I jokingly suggested to a friend that she take a 'catch and release approach' when it comes to dating and sleeping with the younger man she was seeing. They were just having some fun together so I suggested she could teach him a few things and then release him for the benefit of womankind.

When I discussed this approach with my friend Dirk he said, 'Yeah, that's great in theory but our memories are pretty short-term so they'll probably forget most of the lessons.'

This may explain why some older men still believe trying to remove my tonsils with their tongue is great foreplay.

Lucretia Ackfield

Why Men are Like Feral Cats

While some men fit into categories, I've found others share characteristics with the animal kingdom – specifically, feral cats. This statement may seem controversial but in my experience there can be a few similarities.

Do you think I'm too harsh? Men couldn't possibly have anything in common with previously domesticated but now wild animals running the streets with absolutely no sense of responsibility. Could they?

Let me illustrate my point.

When I first met SuperPuss he was a terrified, scrawny black and white cat hiding under my house. I couldn't bear the thought of him being alone and starving so I bought some cat food and thought it would be simple to gain his trust and affection.

I was wrong.

I fed SuperPuss for months but was only allowed to pat him very occasionally while he was eating. After three months, I felt I'd made progress and thought he was ready to sniff my hand. As he gently reached out his paw, I extended my fingers.

Then I felt his claws connect with my skin and knew I'd misread the situation.

A few minutes later he was rolling on his back meowing and showing me his belly as if to say, 'Hey, I feel safe around you and yes, I want you to pat me.' But as I got close he sprinted off and leapt onto the nearest fence where he perched, watching me as he gave himself a good licking.

SuperPuss was a tom and his behaviour shouldn't have surprised me. In my experience males often lure you in and give you a false sense of security before delivering a scratch or two and fleeing the scene. I have no idea why they do this.

It's been a recurring theme in my single life. I'll meet a man who seems interested and interesting. He will seek me out, flirt with me and act like he wants to get to know me better. I'll even check with impartial observers of both sexes to make sure I'm not misinterpreting the behaviour. These observers will invariably agree yes, it seems like the man is interested.

But they always have short attention spans. They'll seem interested one minute, then they leave.

I still haven't solved this problem and clearly I'm missing some critical piece of information. I know they say men are from Mars and women are from Venus[2], but this is getting ridiculous.

Salsa Cat

Latin dance classes might seem an obvious place to meet men with dating potential. After all, you'll be dancing closely together and they like to dance too, so you already have something in common. But in my experience it's unlikely you'll meet your next life partner at a dance class. The nice ones will already have partners. The rest will fall into various categories such as the creepy ones, the emotionally damaged ones and finally, the ones who are perfectly nice but you never want to see them naked.

---

[2] The popular self-help book *Men are from Mars, Women are from Venus* by John Gray was published in 1993 and outlined some of the stark differences between men and women.

The Men I've Almost Dated

There will also be men you really like but of course they will never get it together long enough to ask you out. As Ray, my friend and occasional dance partner once said, 'Dance classes are refuges for the emotionally dysfunctional and needy.' I guess he didn't include himself in this category.

My knowledge of the dysfunctional male and his feral cat qualities has been significantly expanded through several years of dance classes.

It started innocently enough with Salsa Cat. We took a couple of classes together. He was cute and made sure he was in my personal space a lot. Between dance sets, he'd sidle up and stand right up against me. Then he'd stay there, his body touching mine, while the instructor talked. It was unnecessary contact but I let him do it because he was hot. Salsa Cat was the stylish metrosexual type; well-dressed, well-educated and well-liked.

He'd almost give himself whiplash to watch me walk across the room. I'd be at one end of the hall and look up to see him craning his neck to watch what I was doing.

It really was that obvious. He'd be so light-hearted with everyone else but always a little more serious and quiet with me. There were also softly spoken comments like, 'I'll always dance with you'.

But Salsa Cat was inconsistent. We danced together twice a week for 10 weeks but I never knew how each class would turn out. Every time I caught myself thinking he was about to ask me out he'd start avoiding me or flirting his arse off with other women.

I became a mess; a neurotic, insecure, tongue-tied 30-something acting like a teenage mess. Each week I travelled a roller coaster of emotions ranging from excitement and anticipation to pain, hurt feelings and sometimes despair. I'd frequently tell myself that Salsa Cat was nothing more than a lightweight flirt. But it was almost as if he could sense when I'd almost reached the point of no return because, in the next class, he would pay me special attention and I'd be right back where I started.

When I returned from a short two-week break it seemed the situation would finally progress to the next level. 'Did I miss many new steps while I was away?' I asked.

The Men I've Almost Dated

'I'm more interested in knowing if you missed me,' he said.

A beat passed. 'Yes, and I think you know that,' I said. There was a moment of unnecessary but intense eye contact. Tension was in the air. We were in a crowded room but it seemed like we were the only two people there.

The class continued and I felt sure Salsa Cat would ask me out that night. It was going to happen. I changed back into my street shoes really slowly and then dawdled on my way to the exit. I wanted to give him plenty of opportunity.

But he didn't approach so I went home. He spent the following night flirting his arse off with every other woman in the room.

Two weeks later I was teasing Salsa Cat, bumping his foot with mine and just fooling around. 'You're in my personal space,' he stated flatly. He was serious and it was clear he wanted me to stop.

I was crushed. Salsa Cat had been in my personal space repeatedly and unnecessarily for weeks. He'd come on to me and given off all the signs he was interested.

Now I was in his personal space?!

Lucretia Ackfield

I threw myself on the bed that night and shed hot tears of frustration and disappointment. I was terribly hurt. Then anger started to bubble up inside me. A couple of days later I did something I had never done as a single woman before – I told a man he'd upset me. Instead of just taking it, blaming myself and feeling like crap, I stood up for myself and said it wasn't good enough.

Actually, let's face it, I completely lost my temper and acted like a crazy person.

Salsa Cat bore the brunt of years of singledom involving game-playing, non-committal and dishonest men.

I kept as far away from him as possible during the next class– that's quite a feat when you're dancing salsa. At the end of the our first dance I very particularly and noticeably disengaged my fingers from his and moved on to the next dance partner, and then the next and so on around the circle of about 20 men. A few minutes later we were opposite each other again. My anger was palpable and visible in every line of my body.

'What's wrong?' he asked.

The Men I've Almost Dated

'I'd just hate to invade your personal space,' I said sarcastically. Then we changed partners.

He wasn't so cheerful by the time we danced together again. 'I don't know what your problem is. But I'm not doing anything,' he ground out. I somehow restrained myself from punching him in the nose and flounced off to the next partner. I danced my way around the circle, forcing a smile for everyone else and continued to fume.

He was apologising as soon as I was within earshot. 'I'm sorry,' he said. 'I know my behaviour must have seemed a bit hot and cold.'

'Yes,' I said, 'It has been.' Then I moved on to the next partner.

The class finished a few minutes later but he didn't seek me out to explain further. Instead he retreated to his group of friends and watched me nervously, casting sideways glances in my direction as I walked out the door.

He didn't show up for end-of-term classes the following week. I guess he felt like an idiot and didn't want to face a psycho dance partner again. Or maybe his absence had nothing at all to do with me.

It was a month before I saw him again and this time he did seek me out after class. He sat down beside me while I talked to two of our classmates, Dave and Ken. But Dave and Ken didn't get the hint that they should move on and I couldn't just end the conversation abruptly without being impolite. So I was stuck.

I guess Salsa Cat got sick of waiting because he got up and left after a minute or two. I'd started seeing someone else by that point so I didn't run after him. We would dance together over the following years but he never gave me any further explanation. To this day, I'm still not sure what he was thinking.

We've had a few more confused interactions since then. He's been annoyed when other men flirt with me, acted hurt if I don't go out of my way to chat to him and is always seeking me out at social events.

A couple of years later, after a particularly intense period of conflicting signals, I decided to lay it on the line. It was my birthday weekend and I was going to get a straight answer. I turned up at a dance party and told him I'd come specifically just to see him.

He looked at me dumbly for a moment then said, 'I have a girlfriend.'

'Why didn't you say something?' I asked incredulously.

'You never asked.'

People were looking our way so we danced together as normal – at least from the outside it looked normal. On the inside I was losing it. I couldn't just storm out without turning heads so I gave myself a limit of five more dances before I could gracefully exit.

I tried to avoid Salsa Cat for the duration. It was a big dance hall and it shouldn't have been difficult but he kept seeking me out. He asked me to dance three more times that night. I said yes to keep up appearances and then he'd instigate a 'normal' conversation about the weekend, the dance and so on. Anyone with an ounce of sense would have stayed the heck away from me.

I don't know how I held it together.

I declined his third offer to dance. He wished me happy birthday – un-fucking-believable – and I made a swift exit.

Somehow I made it to my car and sobbed the whole way home.

My friend Katie said I'd escaped an emotional nightmare. 'If he's like that now,' she said, 'What would he be like in three months when you're really emotionally involved?'

Why do friends always see these things more clearly that I do?

Shady Cat

There's another type of feral cat. It's the one who tries to get his leg over anything that doesn't have a penis. It's amazing how some men will demonstrate this behavior with absolutely no fear or care for the consequences.

Men in relationships can be the worst culprits.

James made his move while his partner was only metres away. We were having drinks at a mutual friend's place when James started giving a few hints about what was on his mind. It took me a while to catch on to his motives.

We'd met socially a few times and had talked about innocuous subjects. I'd never thought he was interested in me sexually and had definitely not flirted with him. He was in a relationship and not my type. He'd also acted like a nice, normal guy.

But when his partner and the others went into the next room for a few moments, he became all touchy feely and kept trying to hold my hand. What did he think this was, a date?

James also kept refilling my glass and was trying to get me as drunk as possible. Later, he insisted on walking me out before propositioning me just as I reached the front door. 'We could get together you know,' he said quietly while looking deep into my eyes.

'I really don't think that would be a good idea,' I said.

'You know you're killing me. Right?' he said in quiet and deliberate undertone. There was no mistaking his meaning or intention. I definitely wasn't imagining the situation.

'Go and make love to your wife,' I replied. All I could think was, 'Oh my God I can't believe this is happening and please get away from me.' I then hurried down the footpath, threw myself into the waiting taxi and got the heck out of there.

James was definitely a Shady Cat, disguised as a nice guy. At least when they're obvious I can be prepared. But Shady Cats throw me every time because I don't see them coming. Since then, I've avoided James as much as possible. I sometimes wonder if his partner knows the truth about him. But I definitely won't be the one to tell her.

Shameless Cat

Some men are Shameless Cats. They will chat up multiple women in the same location, within minutes of each other. A Shameless Cat doesn't need to be drunk to try this approach because he is single-minded and subtlety is not his first language.

I was standing in a friend's front yard watching the moonrise with a group of neighbours when Joel asked my friend Josie out. She declined. A few minutes later Joel asked me out. Unfortunately, his lack of finesse was glaringly obvious as we were all standing near each other. Joel was completely sober.

The situation got a little more interesting because he asked if I'd meet him at a particular venue (Josie had escaped that part of the invitation). He asked me to meet him at a local pub to watch a football game on Friday night. Apparently he was going to be there with his mates. Seriously? I'm sure every girl would love to meet a man she barely knows in a pub to watch football with a bunch of blokes she has never met. Did I mention he was married?

I politely declined his invitation.

A friend later mentioned the pub was a topless bar on a Friday night. What kind of girl did he think I was?

Never-Been-Faithful Cat

Sebastian said he'd never been faithful to a woman. We were in a dance class together and it was one of those 'unusual' conversations I often find myself in.

He told me his partner felt insecure because there always seemed to be other women around, contacting him, texting, emailing, and so on. But Sebastian said he was just misunderstood. I shook my head (on the inside) as he stared down at me with his big brown eyes. 'I'm so misunderstood, please understand me,' they blinked.

Sebastian was a charming Never-Been-Faithful Cat. He would flirt and behave like

the most unattached man with any attractive
woman within a five-kilometre radius.
If I was his partner, I would have felt
insecure too.

Urban folklore says a man can change his
character with the love of a good woman. So
I'm sure a lot of women would meet a
Never-Been-Faithful Cat and think he was a
challenge. They might even believe they
were the right woman to make him realise
monogamy is the answer to his search for
true happiness. But it's more likely the
'challenge' will leave the woman with her
heart shattered, like so many others
before her.

A Never-Been-Faithful Cat might change
but, in my experience, that only happens if
it's in his best interests and above all, if he
wants to. I also believe that type of change
is best made without another vagina on
the horizon.

The Men I've Almost Dated

The Dating Game

I'm not a successful dater. There have been long tracts of time throughout my thirties when it was more likely you'd find me sitting in a café writing about being single than sharing a drink with a gorgeous man.

'What if I missed him? What if I was supposed to walk across the room and talk to that guy at the party? Should I have smiled less, grinned more or winked at him? Should I have worn a shorter dress, shown more cleavage or covered my knees?'

I've had all these and many less rational thoughts when it comes to thinking about the impressions I make on men. In more optimistic moments I've decided that it's simply not my time yet. My fabulous man is still coming – he's just running a little behind schedule. I'm often late so why wouldn't the love of my life also be tardy?

A few years ago, I met a Belgian backpacker called Kristian who gave me

Lucretia Ackfield

hope that my next love wasn't far away. Kristian was in his late thirties and also searching for love. However, perhaps disappointingly for him, I wasn't looking for love in his direction. We met at a hostel in Croatia and, as travelers often do, we freely shared information about our lives and loves with the knowledge that in a day or two we would move on and never meet again (except possibly on Facebook).

Kristian believed we all have more than one soul mate in the world. 'If I could meet one soul mate [my previous love] around the corner in my hometown then there must be many more soul mates waiting for me across the whole world,' he said.

It was an intriguing thought. Did I have more than one possible soul mate out there? Or is someone only your soul mate for a particular moment in time before you move on to someone and somewhere else?

A cynical part of me thinks you only believe you're with your soul mate until the day you realise you're not. That's the day the sound of them chewing cereal drives you nuts and you discover you never, ever want to see them naked again.

The Men I've Almost Dated

Most of us want to meet our soul mate right now. That's why I date. I want to find my soul mate; that one special person who can fill my world with love and light. But I don't know how those girls in *Sex and the City* did it because sometimes it's a struggle to find a man who will ask me on a date, let alone go out a couple of times, have sex and attempt a relationship.

It was during that same trip to Croatia that I sat on a beach and watched a group of teenage boys trying to get the attention of some teenage girls. The girls were hanging out, giggling, talking and sneaking looks at the boys. The boys were showing off their sporting prowess by kicking a ball around in the surf.

Eventually one of them 'accidentally' kicked the ball close to the girls and of course he had to retrieve it and strike up a conversation. Successful contact was made and soon all the girls were talking to all the boys.

A lot of grown-ups use a similar approach.

A man wants the attention of woman so he uses a tactic to highlight his good qualities - great muscles, stylish outfit, successful business prowess, dancer extraordinaire. The woman is impressed; the man starts a conversation and asks the woman out. It's a simple but civilised approach.

However, sometimes the grown-up male approach can resemble a bad schoolyard accident like when a teenage boy accidentally kicks a ball into a girl's face and breaks her nose.

*

Some male friends think they can obtain the girl of their dreams by stealth. They believe if they hang around long enough as a good friend, the woman will eventually see them as a great choice for a romantic partner. Apparently, once she really gets to know him she will fall into his arms. I called this the 'stealth method' and it relies on the idea that a woman cannot immediately grasp how great a man is. We need to be coaxed into seeing the fabulousness of the man in front of us. Apparently.

The stealth method usually fails. Most women can decide for themselves if a relationship is a friendship or a potential partnership. We don't usually take months to work this out.

But some men don't believe this. Even when I've repeatedly advised male friends that the stealth method is inherently flawed, they still believe they can achieve a different outcome. They are sure the woman they want will eventually appreciate all their wonderful qualities, their sense of humour, their reliability and their sensitivity.

They're right of course. Those women will appreciate their wonderful qualities. But they still won't feel like tearing off their clothes and saying, 'Take me now!'

This male self-delusion often causes problems for women because we like our male friends. They provide us with insights into the frequently incomprehensible male psyche. But the minute we think you want to jump the fence into potential partner territory we're going to back off and no longer be quite so available for Facebook chats, texting and friendly dinners.

*

Unfortunately, some men find it impossible to approach a woman without creeping her out. These men simply don't understand there is a right and a wrong way to approach the opposite sex.

My friend Tara and I were hoping to avoid the wrong approaches when we headed out to one of Brisbane's gay bar institutions. A friendly brunette from western Sydney with a great sense of fun, Tara had been a colleague in my former workplace. We'd met a year earlier and, as our circle of single friends was rapidly diminishing, we could often be found together. Tara had been single for a year or two and was keen to get back into the game. She also had an unconscious talent for attracting freaks. But the only attention we were expecting that Saturday night were compliments on our shoes and some dance requests from drag queens in 80s sunglasses and polka dot dresses.

Tara returned from the bar late in the evening looking incredulous. A man, let's call him Mr Creepy, had approached her and said she reminded him of his ex-girlfriend. Then he offered to buy her a drink. Unsurprisingly, she declined his offer. I have no idea why he thought that would be a successful pick-up line.

The Men I've Almost Dated

Mr Creepy and Mr Creepier (his lookalike friend) proceeded to follow us around the club. Every time we moved, so would they. The club was three stories high and very crowded. But every time we'd congratulate ourselves on losing the creepy twins, we'd turn around to find them positioned close-by.

We ignored them but they were always there, lurking. It felt like we were under siege and I started wondering if we should go elsewhere. By 1am my tolerance for Mr Creepy's behaviour ran out. We'd just moved to yet another dance floor at the other end of the club when I spotted him out of the corner of my eye and thought, enough is enough.

Tara was feeling a bit rattled by the unwanted attention so I left her on the dance floor and walked purposefully over to Mr Creepy. He was seated on a couch and I leaned over him, looked him in the eye and said very strongly and clearly, 'It looks like you're following my girlfriend and you need to stop. Right now.'

He looked back with an unconvincing expression of confusion and shrugged as if to say, 'I don't know what you're talking about.' I didn't believe that for a minute.

'You've been following my girlfriend around and you need to stop it. Right. Now.' I held eye contact for a moment longer before abruptly turning away and heading back to the dance floor.

I looked over my shoulder to see Mr Creepy hurrying away. We didn't see him or his friend again. I laughed when I recounted the story to Tara and realised I'd implied she was my lover. Perhaps that freaked him out even more. Although for most men, it probably would've been a turn on.

*

My dance classes have also provided interesting examples of men approaching women in completely clueless and inappropriate ways. I guess it's not surprising that Latin dancing breeds confusion between the sexes – the style frequently requires neck to knee body contact while sexy music plays in the background.

During one semester, two of my dance partners decided they would, quite randomly, kiss me on the cheek in the middle of class. On both occasions I'd look up to see my dance instructor looking askance in my direction as if to say, what the heck is going on? I was wondering the same thing.

It wasn't the kind of class where we kissed hello at the start or the end. And we certainly didn't do it in the middle either. I had been getting the impression that both Connor and Ben might have a little crush on me but what happened to asking a girl out for a drink first? Neither man ever asked me out on a date. It was probably just as well I as I had no romantic feelings towards them whatsoever.

While the unexpected public displays of affection took me surprise, they didn't offend me. But the sexually-loaded, lip licking offence by Malcolm a year later definitely did.

Dancing with the Stars[3], a television show featuring B-Grade celebrities was popular at the time and whenever we danced together Malcolm would attempt to mimic

[3] *Dancing with the Stars* was a light entertainment dance show broadcast by the Seven Network in Australia.

the exaggerated flamboyance of the so-
called stars. As part of this act, he would
attempt to spend our dances looking intently
into my eyes. I could imagine a Latin lover
called Julio giving me that look when he is
dying to take me to bed and make passionate
love all night long.

I didn't want to make love with Malcolm.
He was a largish man with short dark hair
and an unappealing manner. He wasn't my
type, he wasn't an intense Latin man called
Julio, and I just wanted to learn some
dance steps. So every week I was politely
tolerant and kept my gaze averted as much
as possible.

When Malcolm realised his intense gaze
wasn't working he tried a different
approach. Or perhaps it was just the next
phase of his seduction plan. Whatever the
rationale, his next actions were bizarre.

We were facing each other as the teacher
gave final instructions before the music
started. Although Malcolm had been giving
me his intense Julio look all night, I wasn't
uncomfortable. It was just another class so I
was polite, avoided eye contact and ignored
his ridiculousness.

The Men I've Almost Dated

As the teacher spoke I could feel Malcolm's eyes on my face and I made the unfortunate mistake of looking up. Then he did something that was definitely not one of his usual moves.

He licked his lips.

Now I don't mean a casual moistening of dry lips with a quick flick of the tongue. Instead his tongue emerged slowly from the corner of his mouth and very deliberately ran itself across the surface of his top lip from one side to the other while he looked intently into my eyes.

I felt like I had stumbled onto the set of some bad 1970's porn flick! I couldn't believe what had just happened and was momentarily struck dumb before recovering enough to give him a look that could've shriveled grass. Then we changed dance partners.

Malcolm slunk away early that night and was absent for the next few weeks.

When he finally returned he kept his distance and, luckily for him, there was no more intense gazing or lip licking in my direction. If he'd tried it again I would have been mentally prepared and inflicted damage on a sensitive part of his anatomy.

*

My emotional personality, combined with an astounding naiveté when it comes to the opposite sex has led me down many dating paths strewn with the landmines left by damaged, self-involved and careless men. I usually get too involved too quickly and find myself standing in the street with a bleeding heart (metaphorically speaking) and a sense of confusion a short time later.

My friend Jamie once gave me some advice on how to avoid man-related pain and heartbreak. Although we'd separated from our husbands within a year of each other, Jamie had moved on to a new man and marriage while I was still floundering in the single wasteland.

I was recounting my latest romantic disaster when she said, 'Lucretia, you've got to find a way to maintain your self-preservation. I know you're an emotional person, but you go through so much inner torment with these men.'

'But how?' I asked. 'How do you stop yourself feeling what you feel? For me, once

The Men I've Almost Dated

I've fallen for someone, that's it. I just know the game is over. Didn't you feel that way with Kevin?' I asked. Kevin was her new husband.

'Yes,' she conceded. 'But I had to go through a lot of bastards first. In the end I just played the game like a man to protect myself. I told myself to think like man and don't get too attached until I'm sure.'

*

I've tried to implement Jamie's advice but I'm definitely still a work in progress.

For a long time, whenever a friend or work colleague offered to set me up on a blind date, I'd back away hastily saying, 'Thanks, but no thanks.' Accepting the offer felt like pity and the idea of being thought of as the 'single loser' filled me with horror.

I'd catch myself thinking, 'What kind of guy could he possibly be, this single-loser who can't get a date on his own?' I knew some people might think I fell into that category too. But I knew I didn't belong there. Okay, maybe I was single but I definitely wasn't a loser.

It was this last realisation that eventually changed my mind about blind dates. Perhaps some guy vetted by a friend or colleague might be like me and not a loser? So after nearly five years of single life with only occasional dates or short-lived relationships, I said yes to a blind date. Once my colleague Dana had fallen off her chair in shock, she picked herself up and it was arranged.

Jim and I chatted on the phone and it went well. He had a warm manner and a great sense of humour so we were off to a good start. After chatting for around 20 minutes, we arranged to meet at a coffee shop halfway between where we both lived on the following Saturday.

When he walked into the coffee shop I felt optimistic.

I didn't want to immediately rip his clothes off but he looked nice. He had potential. He was tall, Italian and fit (all pluses), an accountant (not so interesting), and well-travelled, funny and charitable (all pluses again). We also discovered we had a lot of common interests.

I left on an overseas holiday the following week but we kept in touch and Jim was obviously keen to meet again on my return. I'd been single for a long time and

The Men I've Almost Dated

Jim ticked a lot of boxes for me. But there were two glaring issues. He'd admitted to using pot to relax and had a distinct aversion to having children. These were two of my deal breakers but I'd been alone for so long that I almost decided to dismiss them. I walked around Italy thinking, maybe he could give up pot and maybe I won't want children anyway. But my realism finally kicked in and I sent him a message saying I wasn't interested in taking things further. It was disappointing but our date did leave me with hope there were nice single men still out there.

My next blind date was instigated by Wendy, my acupuncturist. 'I have a client who might be a nice friend for you,' she said. 'You could keep each other company.'

I'd known Wendy since before my separation and trusted her judgement. But it took a few more appointments before my nervousness dissipated and I agreed to an introduction. A month later I hurried into the clinic, late as usual, and was greeted by two faces turned expectantly in my direction. Both Wendy and Damien, my erstwhile suitor, were seated in the waiting room awaiting my entrance.

I mumbled an awkward, 'Hi'. Wendy hadn't told me about her planned introduction and all I could think was, 'Thank God I freshened up my makeup before leaving work'. As they stood, I noticed Damien was quite good looking. He said, 'Hello' while Wendy looked on happily. We all stood there awkwardly for a few more seconds. Then he left. After all, we could hardly exchange numbers in that situation, could we?

Two months later Damien called and invited me out for coffee (Wendy had passed on my details with my approval).

I thought the date was going okay but I guess he didn't. His mobile rang after 20 minutes and he left the table to take the call. I suspected it was a friend calling to provide him with an excuse to leave. To be honest, Damien wasn't really my type but is it really such a challenge to sit for 30 minutes and have coffee with someone without checking or answering your phone?

I thought his behaviour was kind of rude and, instead of sitting at the table idly staring into space and feeling stupid, I got out my notebook and started writing. When he finally returned to the table and asked what I was doing, I told him about my book.

He didn't seem comfortable with the idea that he might be included. Then he gave me some excuse about needing to inspect a house (at least that was original) and left. I never heard from him again.

*

In late 2011, I decided I needed to explore another facet of the single life – speed dating. Tara was my wingman and took it very seriously. She was texting me about possible outfits and spray tans even before I'd clicked the online purchase button. I declined the spray tan offer as the orange and slightly jaundiced look isn't flattering for my skin tone.

I had zero expectations for the night. In my mind it was purely a research activity and this attitude certainly helped take the pressure off. I didn't feel nervous at all. Tara on the other hand, had my share of nerves and arrived late due to several last-minute outfit changes.

Lucretia Ackfield

We were two hot, 30-somethings in the basement of a city nightclub hoping to meet the next love of our lives. Our surroundings weren't exactly classy and the carpet was sticky from countless spilled drinks but you never know where love will turn up.

We met 15 men that night and spent four and a half minutes with each of them. All the women sat in one spot while the men rotated around us. Tara and I made an effort to be as approachable as possible. We laughed at the right moments, tried to be interesting and encouraged the men to feel comfortable and chatty.

But we were still sitting in a dimly lit and slightly seedy bar, talking to complete strangers for only a few minutes before they moved on and marked comments on their dating cards.

We had cards too; little pink ones which by the end of the night included handwritten comments like, 'Definitely not', 'Tattoos', 'Engineer', 'Maybe' or 'No!'.

There were a lot of engineers there that night. A number of sheet metal workers and boiler makers were also in attendance along with a flashy architect with an expensive watch who insisted on sitting next to each girl instead of on the chair opposite like everyone else. He fancied himself just a little too much and made most of us feel uncomfortable.

'Where would you most like to visit?' a beefy fitter and turner called Mick asked me. 'Italy,' I responded.

'I'm not a fan of Italy,' Mick said flatly. 'Italian men have no shame in approaching women who are already taken. I was there a couple of years ago with my girlfriend and they were hitting on her right in front of me!' Mick was incensed by this audacious behaviour.

'Maybe Aussie blokes could take a leaf out of the Italian rulebook by taking a risk and approaching a girl without waiting for a written invitation,' I said matter-of-factly. Mick's expression indicated he wasn't going to be asking me for a date anytime soon. The bell rang and he moved on huffily to the next girl who just happened to be Tara.

Unfortunately for him, she also loves Italy.

Another man called Mark likened the experience to being interviewed multiple times. He wasn't enjoying himself and confessed, 'I'm using tonight to dip my toe back in the water after a break-up. I thought I might try to get back into the swing of things but it's bloody uncomfortable.' Others struggled to make conversation and it was easier for me to make them feel at ease than reveal too much about myself. They walked away knowing very little about me but I knew a whole lot about them.

I only identified one romantic possibility but the attraction wasn't mutual. My speed dating venture was a bust.

Tara heard from one of her matches two months later. They went out a few times and he never made a move – didn't even hold her hand. Then he propositioned her one night in a car park and suggested she come home with him. Tara found the abruptness of the invitation and the fact he was living with his father to be a turn-off so she declined. She didn't hear from him again.

Online Freaksters

I had my first boyfriend in Grade 5. His name was Jack and he asked me out through a friend. I said yes and we went out for a couple of months. He even gave me a lovely gold necklace with hearts on it for Christmas. It was my first present from a boy.

Unfortunately, he dumped me three days later. I guess he didn't want to tie himself down during the Christmas holidays.

Jack and I never spoke directly to each other while we were dating. Instead I remember awkwardly smiling at him across the playground while my friends nudged each other and grinned. His mates would do the same. Sometimes we'd all play catch-chasey together but somehow Jack never managed to catch me. He never even came close.

It wasn't a mature relationship.

By the time I reached my late teens it was the late 1980s/early 1990s and dating involved a little more personal contact. It

145

usually started with a conversation at a party or another social event before progressing to a phone call and a date.

But dating in the 2000s isn't as simple. Now we connect through a maze of text messages; Facebook likes, status updates and private messages; tweets; discussion forums; online dating sites; emails; and a range of other electronic mediums.

It's a curious and sometimes disturbing mix of the personal and impersonal. I may never hear a man's voice or see his photo, but I'll be privy to levels of intimacy that 10 years ago, would never be revealed on a first date. Perhaps I'm old fashioned but I don't want learn about your sexual preferences or reveal mine before I actually meet you in the flesh, with your clothes on.

The world of online connection leads us to reveal more than ever before. It creates a false intimacy between strangers that can be misconstrued. My words and thoughts can be expressed as quickly as I type them. But they're often dispatched with little context. Without the inclusion of facial expressions or voice intonations, confusion and misinterpretation can rear their ugly heads before you can say the words 'chat room'.

My interactions with Bernard provide an excellent insight into this dilemma.

I had no romantic intentions towards Bernard. We knew each other socially and I was sitting at home feeling bored when he sent me a Facebook friend request. 'Why not?' I thought. So I accepted and we started chatting online.

I'd never done anything, or at least nothing I was aware of, to make him believe our relationship would evolve past friendship. During our online chats I frequently talked about being single and the kinds of men I met. I also complained about being single and made all the right commiserating comments when Bernard said he was still recovering from his last break-up.

For the record, when a man confides that he's still getting over his ex and feeling a lot of pain, I will commiserate and offer encouraging words. That's my natural empathetic reaction to anyone who's going through a difficult time. But that does not mean I am interested in them romantically.

When he tells me how much his ex hurt him and all the things he misses about her, I do not feel turned on. I will say comforting words such as, 'I'm sure the right person is out there for both of us. We just have to be patient.' But this doesn't mean I want him to proposition me. I don't want to date someone who is still getting over their ex.

Unfortunately, Bernard misinterpreted our conversations and suggested we meet up. I declined as sensitively as possible and said I thought he was great but only viewed him as a friend. When he later admitted to feeling embarrassed for misinterpreting the situation I said, 'Don't worry about it. We'll just be friends and move on.'

But Bernard said he'd rather not explore the 'just friends' route with someone he was attracted to. I thought this was reasonable under the circumstances.

However, his next comments weren't quite so congenial. He advised me not to complain to straight guys (who seemed interested in me) about being single if I wasn't interested in dating them. He said it sent conflicting messages and I should reserve that for my gay friends and the girls.

The Men I've Almost Dated

Suddenly it seemed his misinterpretation was entirely my fault and I had led him on. In my opinion, Bernard's parting comments seemed a little bitchy and lacking in maturity. My response was brief and non-confrontational.

ME: Interesting point Bernard, thank you. For a girl we think it sends the completely opposite message. Ah...men and women are so very different in the way we see the world.

Ciao

Later I wondered why I was so polite in return. A more appropriate response would have been, 'Listen mate, if I was interested in you the last thing I'd do is confess to being a sad sack who hasn't had a date in months and was talking to you online on a Saturday night. And by the way, I'm not interested in dating a man who's not over his ex and is still talking about how much she hurt him. If I'm interested I will mention I'm single but I won't complain about it. I would never in a million years think that was an effective way to attract a man. I'm pretty sure that most women would think the same.'

Lucretia Ackfield

It seems some men, like Bernard, have a different perspective on things. It really is a miracle anyone ever gets together at all.

*

Facebook stalking and chatting has become the norm for single and coupled people. It's not unusual to receive a Facebook friend request from a school friend you haven't seen in 20 years or a colleague you worked with two years ago.

Most of the time, if the request seems reasonable, I accept it and think nothing more about it. I know people with hundreds of Facebook friends, mostly people they barely know. But some men will use this casual Facebook approach to hide their real intentions.

When I received a Facebook friend request from Charlie, it took me a while to work out how we knew each other. But after a brief chat online I realised he was Meg's husband. Meg and I had worked together years earlier but had fallen out of touch after she had children and moved away.

When I accepted his request I assumed Charlie was just one of those people who liked to friend everyone he'd ever met or that he and his wife simply had a joint Facebook page.

I was wrong.

Over a few short messages Charlie revealed he and Meg were still living together until they decided to either get divorced or get back together.

Our correspondence was innocuous and innocent. But I did think it was odd that he'd tracked me down on Facebook. We'd only met once or twice and that was years earlier. And he was still living with his wife.

Our conversation petered out as these things often do. But two months later Charlie did something that made me uncomfortable and revealed his contact probably wasn't as innocent as I'd thought.

I received a birthday text message from an unidentified number on my birthday.

CHARLIE: Hey there Lucretia, Happy birthday. Wishing you a glorious and beautiful day!! Charlie. ☺

ME: Thanks so much for the lovely birthday wishes☺ May I ask which Charlie this is?

Lucretia Ackfield

CHARLIE: Hi Lucretia, it's Charlie, Meg's ex-husband. I know there's a lot of us Charlie's around. We're hard to keep track of ;-) I'm glad you got the message, thought you might have changed your number by now. It's been a while since I've used it, in fact I forgot it was in my phone.

As soon as I read the last message my alarm bells finally started to kick in. I'd never given Charlie my number. He could only have obtained it from his soon to be ex-wife who he was still living with; he'd have to copy it from her phone without her knowledge or he'd found it in the list used to broadcast the news of their baby's birth, years earlier.

Either way, the thought that he'd now used that number to contact me and was escalating contact from a fairly impersonal online channel to my mobile bothered me a lot.

I felt somehow, even though we'd drifted apart, I was betraying Meg and it bothered me that Charlie may have gone through her phone to get my number. I also wondered if he'd been thinking about me years ago when

The Men I've Almost Dated

I first met him and he was still married. It all felt a bit icky.

It felt like he'd contacted me under false pretenses and I deleted him from my friends list. The casual intimacy of Facebook had lulled me into thinking the situation was innocent when it clearly wasn't.

*

I've never liked the thought of online dating. I've always wished for something more natural and organic than matchmaking via an electronic medium. But these days everyone is online. So I eventually had to give in and try it.

It was my friend Marion who introduced me to the idea of online dating. She'd recently ended her dysfunctional marriage and I'd been single for just under a year. We were hanging out on a Friday night when, after a few glasses of wine, she convinced me to peruse some of the dating websites.

I wasn't impressed with the selection.

Some men looked like axe-murderers. Seriously, a smile and friendly appearance is very appealing to women but looking like a prison escapee is unlikely to get you a date. Others had simply taken an old photo and

Lucretia Ackfield

cropped their previous wife or partner out of the shot. We could still see part of her head or her arm on one side.

Men even used their old wedding photos. While this showed the man could make the ultimate commitment it also indicated he was too lazy to make the smallest effort and take a new photo. When a woman is asked, 'When did you first see Carl?' she doesn't want to say, 'Um, it was online and I could see part of his wife's wedding dress and hair.'

Appalling profile names like 'Terrylicious' were also a turn-off and after viewing these gems I drove home thinking I'd rather be single.

A few years later, and still single, I decided to try again. Almost every single person I talked to had been online at least once and some friends were dating or married to people they'd met through dating sites. My plan was to go online for one month only. I had zero expectations of meeting someone but, deep down, that little optimist in my heart jumped up and down and hoped the Universe might deliver a wonderful man into my lap.

154

The Men I've Almost Dated

I signed up for a new and much-hyped dating website and completed the extensive questionnaire to help the computer match me to a suitable partner. The initial profile took an hour to complete followed by hundreds of other optional questions. It took me hours and the whole process felt intrusive. Putting my profile online made me feel like a pork chop in a butcher's window. I felt so awkward and the idea of meeting someone through a one-dimensional visual medium didn't feel natural at all.

The website even gave tips on how to behave during the dating process. One suggested you should take your time to make a decision about a man and implied that you should make the man 'work for it'. Yes, it really did say that. Good to know they don't encourage game playing!

The next day I logged in to find I had seven matches. They all seemed nice but I had no desire to see any of them naked. I wondered if that made me superficial. I knew it would be politically correct to get to know them first as a person rather than judge them on their appearance. But, while I'd heard stories about people who were friends first and then the attraction grew, I thought those occasions were rare – or maybe urban myths.

When you meet someone you usually know within the first 30 seconds if you would ever be interested in seeing them naked. You have to find them visually appealing in some way – a smile, a body shape, eyes, etc. If the thought of seeing them naked leaves you feeling cold, then it's probably never going to happen. You can't force it. Online dating makes this kind of assessment difficult but I guess you have to go with your first impressions.

My friend Andie had recently married someone she met online and offered me her perspective. 'Online dating is like a business,' she said. 'If they don't make the grade show them the door; you don't have time to muck around.'

My search continued.

My profile information was fairly succinct. I wanted to provide enough to give them a taste of who I was but not my entire my life story. I didn't want a complete stranger to know everything about me. That seemed a little risky and unwise. And I was definitely not answering the question about how high my sex drive was. Shouldn't we at least hold hands before getting to that level of intimacy?

My minimalist approach was uncommon and, once my matches started arriving, I was amazed at how much men were prepared to reveal about themselves. The standard profile questions required responses about everything from your personal strengths to how friends perceived you.

One question asked, 'What are you passionate about?'

One man said he liked to maintain a high standard of personal grooming and give compliments to his partner. He seemed okay but I did wonder if he'd have more skin products than me.

Another question asked for details about the first thing people noticed when they met you.

Quite a few men took this as a green light to highlight their physical highpoints with one man describing his alternative hairstyle, professional presentation and the fact he had a great tan. I figured this last attribute could be a strong selling point with some women but I did wonder if he'd heard about the dangers of skin cancer.

The most hilarious response was to a question which asked, 'What is the most important quality you are seeking in a partner?'

This attracted one man's very profound response indicating his preference for a woman who looked hot in a pair of jeans. Was I wrong to desire a little more depth in the man I was seeking? I moved on. Needless to say, I really had to question why the computer matched me to these men.

One man did look interesting and I agreed to meet him for a date. Derek was a passionate teacher with an Italian background. Our first date progressed from a planned drink to an unplanned dinner and movie. We laughed, had things in common and it was clear he didn't want the date to end. He was also kind of cute.

When he asked me out for dinner for the following Saturday night I said yes.

We met at a local bar and it wasn't a good sign when he confessed to flinging his chewing gum into the gutter just as I got out of the cab. When he'd removed his shoes and socks during the movie on our previous date, I'd thought it was quirky. But throwing his gum onto the footpath for someone to wear as an unwanted shoe ornament just seemed disrespectful.

We settled into a table for two, he ordered me a glass of wine and we chatted about our day. He mentioned that he'd been to see the movie *Underworld: Awakening* and how much he loved the 3-D effects. Then he said he was hanging out for 3-D porn.

His words hung in the air for a moment before plummeting to the ground. I told myself he was joking and changed the subject. After all, we've all said stupid things at the wrong moment and maybe he was just nervous. The conversation seemed to get back on track and I started telling him about my blog, lucyandlife.com

'What's the point of blogging?' he asked. For a moment I thought there was a hint of disparagement in his tone but then thought no, that would be crazy. After all, why would someone who had never read my work ever disparage it? So, I told him it was about the discipline of writing and we talked about the book I was developing (yes, this book!).

Things went further downhill.

I said I was writing about my own life and hoped people could relate to the things that had happened to me. 'Nobody wants to see a movie or read about someone who is like them,' Derek said. 'They want to escape.'

I asked some questions just to clarify his meaning. Surely I was misinterpreting him? But no, I wasn't. He didn't think that anyone would want to read my work as it would be too much like their own lives. His comments were similarly offensive and unsupportive during the short walk to the restaurant. When we sat down at the table, surrounded by loud Mexican décor and similarly loud band, he said, 'You look confused.'

'I'm perplexed,' I said. 'You seem to have a good heart but you keep saying things that are likely to offend me.'

'You're too sensitive,' he replied dismissively as he browsed the menu. 'If I don't say what I think there will be nothing to say.' Then he laughed.

The Men I've Almost Dated

We didn't talk a lot during dinner and he continued to act like everything was completely normal. During some strained chitchat, he made the comment that he often offends people. 'Why do you think that is?' he asked.

'Maybe you should consider the feelings of the person you're talking to,' I said quietly. My answer seemed to wash over him.

Incredibly, I was polite to this man throughout our meal because I've been raised to have good manners. I also kept thinking maybe I was misinterpreting his words. Derek said on our first date that he always tells his students they can do anything and encourages them to follow their dreams. When I compared this to his comments about my writing, he said, 'I just wouldn't want someone to waste their time.'

I sat there sucking down my sangrias like there was no tomorrow and thinking, 'I need to get really drunk really quickly or I'm going to throw this drink in his face'.

When the waitress finally arrived to clear our plates I declined her offer of dessert. I was hoping to end our 'date' as soon as possible. I put 'date' in inverted commas because dates are supposed to be pleasurable and this was definitely not.

But Derek went ahead and ordered dessert for us to share. 'You'll like it,' he said. Then he brought up my book again and said, 'No one wants to read another *Sex and the City*,' then began laughing when he saw the expression on my face. 'Ha ha, that's what you're aiming for isn't it?' he said, and then he laughed some more.

I was shocked. Could his behaviour be any more atrocious? What a complete and utter jerk.

Often when I'm confronted with an insensitive and rude person I will continue to smile, be polite and pretend that everything is fine. But this time I chose a different road.

I excused myself and went to the bathroom. As I rifled through my purse I realised I didn't have the right change to simply fling the cost of my dinner on the table and stalk out. 'Do you have change for a 50?' I asked a woman as she exited a stall. 'No sorry,' she said before washing her hands and briskly leaving the room. She probably thought I was a bit crazy.

I followed her out and stood in the hallway. At one end was the entrance back into the restaurant. The woman I'd accosted in the public bathroom was pushing through glass doors at the other end and walking into the car park.

I watched her leave then looked back towards the restaurant. Then I looked back towards the glass doors, then back to the restaurant again. 'I can't go back in there,' I thought. 'I just can't.'

'Can I just leave?'

My legs began carrying me towards the doors and seconds later I was bursting out into the cool night air. My adrenalin was pumping and I couldn't believe what I was doing. I was terrified of being seen from the restaurant so I ducked and weaved behind parked cars as I made my way towards the main road.

I flagged down a cab, threw myself in and began laughing hysterically. I couldn't believe what I'd done. When the cab driver asked if I'd had a good date, I laughed even more. He joined in when I told him the story.

Although I did laugh about it, I was also really shocked. The whole thing was unbelievable. I sent Derek a message saying, 'Thanks for a not so lovely evening. If you'd like to send me your account details I will transfer you the funds for dinner.' He didn't reply and I had this horrible moment when I thought of him sitting there alone, waiting for me at the table. What if he didn't get my message?

I rang the restaurant but the phone just rang and rang, so I gave up. I figured Derek would get the message either way. I didn't hear from him again and blocked all our communication on the dating site.

He probably felt humiliated sitting there in the restaurant on his own with his dessert for two. But I couldn't really find it in my heart to feel sorry for him. It could have been worse – I could have stained his shirt with my sangria.

I took a break from online dating after that appalling experience. I didn't think I was going to find the love of my life in cyberspace.

The Men I've Almost Dated

Some men are attracted to me; that much is clear. But many lose confidence and flee before making a move. I don't understand why men find it so hard to take the big scary step and ask me out.

I'm attractive, well-presented, articulate, confident and financially independent. I don't expect much from a partner. I don't expect him to provide for me. I just want to go out and have a laugh, have good sex (obviously) and be loved. I also need him to accept me as I am and support me. In return I'll accept and support him.

I'm not desperately seeking a father for my children or a man to 'keep me' in shoes, handbags and jewellery. I can provide those things for myself. I don't even want a high flyer, just someone who is passionate about what he does.

I don't think my expectations are very high but it feels like it's getting harder and harder to get a date. It doesn't help that, after close to 40 years on this planet, I still don't understand men. Despite intensive research and long periods of sustained observation I still don't know what the heck is happening when it comes to the dating game.

There have been so many times when I've thought a man was interested. But then it's become abundantly clear that I was mistaken and they walk away, deny they were ever interested or leave with another girl.

Rohan is an excellent example of a man I've almost dated. We met at a family wedding held interstate. The bride, my cousin Janey, suggested I keep him company. We were both single and he was attractive so I agreed.

Within 15 minutes, I'd learned Rohan was a semi-professional soccer player and how much he was paid for this activity. He volunteered this information. I probably wasn't as impressed as other women because I'm not a soccer fan and am clueless about professional sports generally. I wondered later if that made me an interesting challenge.

The Men I've Almost Dated

Rohan also mentioned he'd been on a couple of dates recently but wasn't sure how serious he was about the woman, so he didn't invite her to the wedding. I thought this was a wise decision and perhaps he was a little more evolved than some of the men I'd met recently. It also seemed to indicate he was still available.

We sat down at a nearby table and continued to chat for the rest of the night. We talked almost exclusively to each other for four hours. Other people dropped by occasionally but we stayed together.

For four hours.

Rohan was extremely attentive. He made sure my glass was always full but it didn't feel like he was trying to get me drunk. Another woman kept looking his way and tried to engage his attention whenever he went to the bar. But he always made his way back to my side.

We discovered we had a lot in common like travelling, books, television shows we liked and more. Sometimes he would say something and it was as if it had come out of my own mouth. We were in sync.

Lucretia Ackfield

There were few of the awkward silences
that characterise many first dates. We made
each other laugh. It was great. He also
mentioned he frequently travelled interstate
(to the city where I lived) to visit relatives
and close friends.

He said he lived not far from where I
was staying.

Rohan held my gaze and reached over to
touch my arm or knee several times when
emphasising a point. It was like we were in
our own little world.

When I returned to the family table at the
end of the night to collect my bag my sister
Nerina asked, 'Are you getting his number?'

'No. He lives here. I live in Brisbane,' I
said. To be honest until that moment I'd just
been having a good time and wasn't really
thinking beyond the night.

'Oh Lucretia. Get his number,' she said.
She may have also made some comment
about me being hopeless. I can't quite recall
but the remark would have been accurate.

I returned to Rohan and stood there
looking up at him. 'I've gotta go,' I said.

'Oh,' he said.

Pause.

The Men I've Almost Dated

I waited for a, 'Can I get your number', 'Can I give you a lift' or 'Do you want to go on for a drink'. But all I heard were the sounds of wedding guests leaving.

'Okay, bye.' I stood on my toes to kiss him on the cheek.

'Bye,' he said.

I turned and walked very slowly across the dance floor towards the exit. I thought I'd give him time to gather his wits and ask me out. But he didn't hurry after me and didn't ask for my number.

When I got to the car my family asked, 'So did you get his number?'

'No,' I said. 'He lives here.' I was feeling kind of stupid.

'That doesn't matter. He goes to Brisbane all the time,' my sister Jasmine said. Clearly they'd been making enquiries of their own.

'Oh, he definitely got her number,' Dad said.

'No I didn't get his number,' I said. 'And he didn't ask for mine.'

There was a moment of confused silence in the car before Mum started talking about what a great wedding it was. It was only while sitting at the airport the next day that I realised just how strange the whole interlude had been. After all, who monopolises a woman's conversation for four hours but doesn't ask her out?

'Noooo,' I moaned with my head in my hands. 'I should've asked for his number.'

Nerina looked at me and shook her head despairingly. 'But he can get my number from Janey. Right?' I asked.

'Of course,' she said.

My cousin returned from her honeymoon a couple of weeks later and I asked, 'Is Rohan gay? Is he in a relationship with someone else?'

'No' was the answer to both questions. But I never heard from him.

Rohan could have asked the bride for my number. They are good friends and she was briefed to provide it to him on request. I also sent him a 'Hey, how are you?' text about a month later just in case he was too shy to ask Janey for my details.

We messaged for an hour or two. It was amusing; it was flirty. He mentioned many of the subjects we'd discussed and laughed about at the wedding. He was on his way to a party and was messaging while driving. Then he arrived at the venue and we said goodnight.

And that was it.

The whole thing was very confusing and I sought advice from my down-to-earth mate, Darren. 'Rohan was either a really shy person who hitched his wagon to yours because you were friendly and gave all the signals of being interested in the process but wasn't, or…he's a pussy,' was his analysis.

My sister Nerina said, 'Yeah that was just weird.'

Three years after the wedding, under the influence of alcohol and mischievous friends, I decided to get to the bottom of the Rohan mystery and the following texting conversation ensued.

ME: Hey there, just having a chat with a few friends, and we're talking about people we met that seemed nice but didn't date. So I'm just wondering, is there a reason you didn't ask me out?! Hope you're well. Lucretia

ROHAN: Hey there, Im well hope u r too.. I didn't ask u out cause us live in Brisbane id had a recent failed long

*distance relationship so even considering
starting up someone living in another state
was out of the question. There ya go*

*ME: Nice one Rohan! That must have
been pre Skype ;)*

*ROHAN: Yeah and pre iPad too he he
Why didn't you ask me anyways lol*

*ME: I'm an old fashioned girl so I was
waiting for u to step up;)*

A man can monopolise your company for
four hours at a wedding, flirt his arse off but
have no intention of asking you out. Weird.
It's probably just as well because his
punctuation was appalling.

*

I also thought the cute guy with
dreadlocks who fixed my endless supply of
stilettoes was going to ask me out. He even
told me of his plans to share his shoemaking
and shoe repair skills by training
disadvantaged people in Africa.

Yes, okay, stop laughing. I thought his
aspirations were very admirable. I was
researching aid work at the time and thought
maybe he could teach his shoe repair skills
and I could teach...something else.

The Men I've Almost Dated

On so many occasions he seemed on the verge of asking me out. He'd pause for a moment too long but at the last minute he would always turn away. I kept dropping by with my shoes but he just never managed it.

Eventually I gave up and took my footwear somewhere else.

*

Some men will make a complete arse out of themselves in their eagerness to get my attention. But still won't ask me out.

The Giggler giggled and flirted so overtly with me during dance class that I was almost embarrassed. Of course I've since realised that I don't want a man who giggles all the time but he was good-looking and I was blinded by his sexy dance moves.

The Giggler sought me out constantly throughout the dance term. He was always the first to grab my hand when we were choosing partners in class. He'd also take a few steps towards me at the end of class then seem to change his mind before rapidly moving in the opposite direction.

I think I rang the death knell for this 'maybe relationship' by doing what I'm sure most dating experts would tell you never to do. At the end-of-term dance party, The Giggler asked me to dance and we chatted about relationships and dating as we moved around the floor. In my foolish naiveté I thought I'd make things easy for him. At the end of the dance, just before we parted ways, I looked him straight in the eyes and said, 'If you ask me, I'll say yes.'

He froze for a moment and made no reply. The memory makes me cringe even now. It was too much honesty for The Giggler.

I saw him two months later flirting with a girl wearing cowboy boots. Perhaps if I'd worn spurs he would have felt more comfortable.

*

Sometimes a man makes his interest in me so obvious and intense that I've thought, 'He'll be chatting me up within the hour'. But even then, it doesn't happen.

Dorian was one of those men. I was shuffling through some speech notes at a workshop when I looked up to see him entering the room. Our eyes locked and my knees almost buckled. The connection was immediate and electric; an arc of energy flew across the room between us.

He made his way to a nearby table and twisted in his seat so he could watch as I continued to set up. He was definitely keeping me in sight at all times.

The workshop ran for two hours and I tried not to let my eyes drift in his direction too often. When the session ended everyone began networking and preparing to leave.

I was saying goodbye to a few people and looked up briefly to scan the room. Dorian was standing in the middle of the hall and staring straight at me. Our gaze held for a few moments. Then someone asked me a question and I had to look away. A few minutes later I looked up to see Dorian strolling out the doors.

I was confused. Why didn't he come over and talk to me? Who stares at someone like that if they have no intention of doing anything about it? It made absolutely no sense and I never saw him again.

*

It was my friend Samantha who suggested Sinesh might be a good housemate for me. You might remember him as the man who turned my regular sweaty, grass covered fight with the lawnmower into a spectator sport with his mate Jimmy.

Samantha had described him as a shy and very polite man from Malaysia who worked with her boyfriend in the mines. Over the phone he sounded short and lightly built.

But the man who walked up my front stairs was a six-foot tall Sri Lankan and one of the most incredibly good-looking men I had ever met. 'Holy crap!' I thought as I managed to contain my hormones and behave like a semi-normal person while he wandered through the house.

Sinesh would be working on-site a lot and would only stay at the house occasionally. As we stood in the backyard to discuss the details he puffed out his chest a little as if he was trying to impress me. I was impressed.

'Was there something you forgot to mention?' I asked Samantha after he left. She giggled over the phone line. 'I thought you'd like something nice to look at around the house,' she said.

The Men I've Almost Dated

Sinesh lived with me for six weeks. I'd walk in the front door at night to find him sitting in the lounge-room, freshly showered and waiting to talk to me. The flirting was intense and after a couple of weeks it became something more.

We only went on one proper date and as we walked back to the car after the movie it felt really awkward. He eventually moved out and on the last night I mused that I was never going to hear from him again. 'Never assume Lucretia,' he said. 'Assumption is the mother of all fuck-ups.'

He never did call.

Clearly my assumption wasn't a fuck up but perhaps he was though. His refusal to remove his shirt and sometimes his socks while having sex was probably a good indication that things weren't going to end well. He also told me at one point that I should, 'Just lie there,' so he could kiss me. Apparently I was meant to be a passive participant in the activity.

Nevertheless, I sent him a text message two months later asking why he never called (this was preceded by one, okay two, letters telling him how much I missed him).

Lucretia Ackfield

'I just didn't know what to say,' he said.

If I want to sleep with a potential housemate in the future, I won't let them move in.

*

I should have learned by now that any man you meet in a dance class is unlikely to ask you out. I should also have learned to stop letting my heart be distracted by men under the age of 30.

When I first met Larry I remember looking up and thinking, what is this hairy goofball grinning at? He had shaggy hair, a three-day growth and was very, very tall with a set of perfect teeth that I found unnerving.

It didn't even register that he was good-looking. I can be a bit slow sometimes.

Over the ensuing weeks we enjoyed dancing together and he would go out of his way to say hello and goodbye to me at every class. He didn't do this with anyone else and he was definitely flirting with me at every opportunity. Classmates even commented on his obvious attentions.

When I asked how old he was, he pretended he couldn't remember.

The Men I've Almost Dated

'Are you so old that you've forgotten?' I asked. 'No,' he grinned. 'It's just that it doesn't matter.'

I was a few years older than him and he knew that. I wondered if he was trying to tell me something.

He disappeared for a couple of weeks and, when he returned, he said he'd been overseas. 'Who did you go with?' I asked. 'By yourself, with a tour...?'

'Caitlin,' he said. Then he didn't say anything else. He didn't say, 'Caitlin my wife, Caitlin my girlfriend, Caitlin my sister, Caitlin my cousin.' He just said, 'Caitlin' and left the word hanging in the air with no further explanation. Was I supposed to know who Caitlin was?

I should have asked. But instead I just changed the subject and we talked about something else. I was annoyed though. I figured Caitlin was a girlfriend he'd been very careful not to mention earlier. Larry kept giving me apologetic looks for the rest of the night.

Two weeks later I had lunch with my friend Anne who, it turned out, was an acquaintance of the hairy goofball. She'd met him at a social function earlier in the year.

'Oh my God Lucretia, he's hot!' she said.

I told her what had been happening and asked if he had a girlfriend. 'I think he did at the time,' Anne said.

'Can you see if you can find out?' I asked, 'If you don't feel compromised by that.'

'Of course,' she said.

A couple of days later I had my answer. 'Nothing definite but he's in the profile photo on this girl's Facebook page and it looks like they could be together,' she said.

My lovely friend was trying to cushion the blow because, when I saw the photo, I knew that it was definite. There was nothing ambiguous about their relationship in the photo.

I was angry then. I also felt terribly hurt and wondered how it could have happened again. Larry was just another man coming onto me when he was already taken. I also realised the girl in the photo was in the class after mine. I'd seen him chatting to her. She was also hot and a lot younger than me.

The Men I've Almost Dated

Larry and I still had classes together so I decided I would let it go, try and keep my distance as much as possible and focus on the dancing.

He didn't seem to like my approach. In fact, sometimes the sexual tension coming from him was almost overwhelming. You could have cut it with a knife. He'd be watching me walk towards him and it was as if everything in him was reaching out to grab me and pull me into his space. Sometimes I felt like, if the room had been empty, he would have pushed me up against the nearest wall and taken me there and then.

I didn't know what was going on.

One night he was sweating up a storm and he apologised because he thought he smelled.

'You should keep your arms down as much as possible then,' I joked. Humour is always my favourite defense mechanism. Then we danced together and he said, 'I guess I'll just have to dance like this then.' He held me very close and barely moved as we danced very, very slowly.

Lucretia Ackfield

'Oh, I'm not going to complain about that,' I said (damn my hormones to hell!). His slow dancing continued for almost the whole song and was completely unnecessary. There were a lot of other moves he should've been practicing.

Term finished a week or two later and I was relieved. Whatever was going on, it was over and I could move on.

But next term both Larry and Caitlin were in my class. I couldn't believe it.

I tried to play it cool. I was polite and distant. But Larry was having none of it. The more I tried to distance myself, the friendlier he became. It was a disaster.

If there had been another class running at my level I would have transferred into it. But there wasn't so I tried to behave normally and failed miserably.

The friendlier he became, the angrier I felt. I just wanted him to get the hell away from me. After a few weeks I was completely fed up and my polite but distant façade had degenerated into a polite but annoyed one. This behaviour bothered Larry so much that he called me on it.

The Men I've Almost Dated

'Do you have a minute after class?' he asked one night as we mastered the latest salsa moves.

I looked at him and thought 'FUUUCCK!!!' I felt like saying no, don't ever talk to me again but, of course I couldn't. I could do passive aggressive but I couldn't do impolite.

'Yep, okay,' I said. The blood was rushing in my ears.

After class I followed him downstairs to the footpath.

'It's obvious that something is bothering you and I want you to tell me what it is,' he said. 'You can trust me. I need you to tell me. We should be able to talk about this,' he said. Why on earth he thought we, two people who really didn't know each other at all, should be able to talk is beyond me.

I wanted to run. In fact, I almost said, 'Doesn't matter, gotta go,' and sprinted up the street. Instead I decided that maybe just once I could trust that a man was genuine and wanted to clear the air.

'How do you think you acted around me last term, Larry?' I asked.

'Um, I don't know?' he looked a little confused.

'You acted like you're single.'

'But I'm not.'

'Yes, I know that,' I ground out. The word 'now' hung unspoken in the air between us.

'And you thought…oh…' I could almost see the wheels turning in his head as he worked it out. 'I'm sorry.'

'Okay.'

'I'm sorry.'

'Okay.'

'If I'd been interested I would have asked you to hang out sometime,' he said. Seriously!

'Sorry,' he said. 'This happened once before, years ago, but I thought I'd sorted it out.'

'Apparently not.'

'Sorry.'

'Okay.'

'I need to reflect on this. Sorry.'

'Okay.'

'Sorry.'

The man was apologising more than any other man I had ever met in my life. 'It's okay. A lot of guys do it, it just gets a bit annoying after a while.'

Our classmates were now spilling out into the street, walking past and casting curious glances in our direction. I'm pretty sure Caitlin had also come downstairs because Larry started looking nervously in that direction. But it was clear that he wasn't leaving until he knew that everything was resolved. I had to admire his bravery, or foolhardiness, in hanging in there. In the crudest language, his approach took 'balls'.

'It's okay,' I said. 'You'd better go. I'll see you next week.'

'Okay?' he asked.

I nodded and he left.

I have no idea how he explained it all to his girlfriend. I expect that was a tricky conversation. As for me, well, it felt like one of the few honest conversations I've had with a man as a single person. It seems that most men can't be honest. It's too confronting and scary. Pathetic really.

When we danced together the following week, Larry was determined to make sure that everything was resolved. 'How are you?' he asked, looking me straight in the eyes. Clearly he wasn't going to let me hide.

'I'm good thanks, how are you?'

'Good.'

'Thank you for what you did the other day, I think it was very brave of you to do that,' I said.

'Thank you for being honest with me,' he said.

We smiled at each other. 'My father says that miscommunication leads to all the problems in the world,' he mused.

'I think he's right,' I said.

Then we talked about other things and everything felt fine because we'd cleared the air and I let it go.

Caitlin wasn't comfortable though and seemed pretty insecure about it all. She would shoot venomous glances my way and Larry would start dancing like the Tin Man whenever she had us in her sights. In my ungenerous moments I thought it served him right. But mostly, I wished that there was some way I could let her know I wasn't interested in another woman's leftovers.

The Men I've Almost Dated

I left it to him to sort it out. Anything I said would probably have made the situation worse.

I later discovered Larry had strong evangelical Christian beliefs and that made me laugh because I am a very non-religious person. It would never have worked.

Was I played? Maybe. I know I didn't imagine any of it but, if it had been intentional, why would he have made such an effort and risked the repercussions from his girlfriend. He seemed completely honest and open when we had that conversation.

It still makes no sense. No wonder I'm still single.

Lucretia Ackfield

Never Ask A Man If He's Gay When…

The first man I had sex with after my marriage ended couldn't get it up. Then he couldn't remember my name. It's a miracle that I ever went 'out there' again.

I'd only been single for a few months when Samantha and I walked into a local haunt known for drunken hookups and footballers. Footballers don't do it for me (I prefer men with necks) and I'd only been single for a few months, so sex wasn't really on my mind. I'm not sure what Samantha was thinking. I'd moved into her place just after my separation and she was about a year ahead of me in the single stakes. She was a good-looking blonde with curves in all the right places and definitely more experience in the art of pick-up.

It was a packed Saturday night - girls in sky-high skirts, footballers, over-dressed groups fresh from formal events in the city, and men and women drinking more than

The Men I've Almost Dated

was sensible. Samantha and I were at the bar when we found ourselves the centre of attention for a group of 20-somethings on the other side of the dance floor. The blonde one kept trying to catch my eye. He had the look of a young surfie barely out of his teens.

To get rid of him I bummed a cigarette from his mate Michael. He worked in asbestos removal and turned out to be quite affectionate.

An hour later we were making out in the backseat of a cab while Samantha rode upfront.

'My bed is unmade,' I whispered urgently to Samantha as we got out of the cab. 'What do I do?'

'Leave it to me,' she said. 'Just give him a beer from the fridge.'

We headed to the kitchen while Samantha raced into my room, frantically made the bed before dashing into her bedroom yelling, 'Goodnight!' as she slammed the door.

She was a great housemate.

I wish I could say what followed was the best sex of my life. I wish I could say he was a great lover. But I can't and he wasn't. Michael couldn't get it up. He was embarrassed and I was mortified.

I lay there thinking there was something wrong with me. Then something inside made me turn and ask, 'You don't even remember my name do you?' He shook his head and I burst into tears. My first one-night-stand was a complete disaster.

I was clueless and unsure of myself. 'Great. I can't even turn a man on enough to get it up,' I thought. I almost put myself on the celibacy bench permanently after the experience.

My sex-life was a non-starter. But of course, it wasn't my fault. Michael had broken up with a long-term girlfriend only three weeks earlier and wasn't ready to see anyone else, naked or otherwise. Thankfully, with a bit more practice, he did recover his mojo and his erection a couple of days later. My faith in sex was restored. His expert kissing style was also a bonus.

Unfortunately, Michael was the first in a long line of limp bedroom situations. I seem to have attracted more than the usual quota in my lifetime. My friends remain optimistic though and always seem surprised when they hear about my latest fiasco in the bedroom.

My friend Carina always waits expectantly to hear the details about my latest crush.

'So?' she'll ask. 'How's it going?' 'He's great,' I'll reply. 'But…he's got that problem.'

'What do you mean?' she'll be puzzled, tilting her head to one side.

I'll raise my forearm 45 degrees before letting it drop limply back on to the table. 'No. Not again!' she'll exclaim. 'How is this possible? Where do you find these men?'

'I don't know,' I will groan despairingly while dropping my head into my hands. 'I don't know.'

Maybe I'm scary when naked and should keep most of my clothes on. Or perhaps I'm intimidating or hideous to look at? It's been a little demoralising but at least my sexual performance doesn't rely on a hard on.

It's incredible how many things can affect the penis. My friend Carrie, who had a penchant for gym junkies, once told me scary stories about steroids and what they could do to romance in the bedroom. Her partner loved to work out and used the drugs to help him build his version of the perfect body.

But, while his muscles got bigger, his erection (if he got one at all) only got smaller. His balls were also shrinking to the size of raisins. Her tale of splinting his penis with her fingers to get it into her vagina did not sound appealing.

Between drugs, alcohol, ageing, emotional and medical issues, I'm just grateful my equipment doesn't rely on something rising to the occasion. I once read that 40 percent of men over the age of 40 would experience some form of erectile dysfunction. It wasn't an uplifting thought. For sexually active women this means, no matter how many men you date, eventually you will probably find yourself holding something limp in your hand and wondering what the hell to do with it.

All this research, anecdotal evidence and personal experience indicates I should be looking for a man who doesn't take drugs, drinks minimally and has no pre-existing emotional or medical issues.

The Men I've Almost Dated

It could be a tricky proposition but I'm keeping the faith.

And, following a recent experience, I'm going to avoid asking a man if he's gay when he's naked, in my bed and can't get it up. A friend had suggested David was gay and the thought had stuck with me. Then I just blurted it out. It did seem reasonable at the time but I don't think he appreciated the question and let's face it, it probably wasn't the most sensitive thing I could've said in the circumstances.

Lucretia Ackfield

The Sex Drought and Casual Casualties

When I first left Daniel, I began searching for a new hobby. My top choices were Latin dance classes or life-drawing. When Marina, my married co-worker, heard about my dilemma she said, 'No, not the life-drawing. Do Latin dancing, just to be held.'

I can remember feeling so angry at her comment that I had to turn away with tears in my eyes. How dare she think I had to be held and that should be a motivator for me. How ridiculous. I was self-sufficient and didn't need a man thank you very much.

But much to my chagrin, Marina was completely right. I've been taking classes ever since and being held is one of the best things about them.

It's not that I want to jump into bed with my dance partners, far from it. Most hold no romantic interest for me whatsoever. But it is truly wonderful to be held close to another human being, a member of the opposite sex, when all other opportunities are temporarily unavailable.

Sex isn't just about the physical act of the penis entering the vagina. It's everything else. It's touching someone and being touched. It's having someone care enough to want to make you feel good and to engage in the most primal and intimate act you can ever experience. It's the feeling of a man's arms around you and the stillness that comes when you feel like, just for that moment, nothing else can touch you. Feeling that connection to another human being reminds you that you are alive. Even if the man does leave a few hours later and is never heard from again.

Living without that intimacy can be challenging. Of course, I've had one-night-stands and some of them have been great. But when the man leaves in the morning, I'm back to square one.

A lot of women use casual sex to fill the gap while waiting for Mr Right. After all, fuck buddies, bootie calls and one-night-stands help you get through those times when there is no one more serious on the horizon.

I've always been envious of women who can have uncomplicated regular weekly or monthly bootie calls with a 'special friend' and then walk away with no regrets or second thoughts. Unfortunately, I'm just not built that way. One-night stands I can do well enough. If you only know someone for a few hours, usually under the influence of alcohol, it's easy to walk away.

But when I've attempted a regular casual arrangement, it has never ended well. The more I get to know them physically, the more I want them mentally. Then it's a slippery, slippery slope to a place where I am no longer in control.

Hindsight invariably shows I was just blinded by sex and didn't see the real person in front of me. I think the scariest thing in those situations was how quickly I began to lose myself. Sex and emotions are inextricably linked for me and therein lies the danger.

Being older has not made me necessarily wiser or more detached when it comes to love.

The Men I've Almost Dated

PART 3
The Lessons of Lucretia

Lucretia Ackfield

The Men I've Almost Dated

My first kiss was with a lovely boy called
Eamon. He was a nice guy but,
unfortunately, he slobbered all over the
bottom half of my face and it was a bit like
kissing a cow. My next boyfriend Calvin, a
friend of Eamon's, tried to remove my
tonsils with his tongue. I felt like gagging
every time.

Things eventually improved in the
kissing department. My now ex-husband
was a great kisser so I didn't have to worry
about tongues and mouths being in places
they shouldn't. When I re-emerged into
single-land I was under the impression that
men became more skilled with age
and practice.

I was wrong.

Two years ago I looked up to find my
date, a 40-year-old man who should have
known better, leaning in towards me with
his mouth open in a large 'O' about the size
of a fifty-cent piece. He was perched on a
bar stool about a metre away and as he
moved in I worried my face would be

consumed by a human-sized goldfish. It nearly was.

Bad techniques seem to spread over into bedroom activities too. For example, I'm still unsure why a man said to me during our first intimate experience, 'I like to watch it go in. Feel free to sort yourself out.'

I'm also unsure why some men haven't realised that giving head is actually a reciprocal activity and it is polite to return the favour. Finally, and this is for any future romantic partners out there, *Deep Throat* was a porn film and slamming your penis into the back of my throat just makes me want to gag and possibly bite you.

Here are some other things I've learned since my separation.

The Dating Drive-through

Some additional facts would have been useful when I began my journey into the land of single. These quick tips could've helped me make wiser decisions about the men I've allowed into my life.

In the absence of a more comprehensive guide, I've developed my own list of dating drive-through tips. They're quick, easy and would have helped me countless times over the past few years. Ignore these at your peril.

1. Small hands do not equal a small penis. This is an urban myth that has cursed many a small-handed man.

2. Good-looking does not equal good in bed. This could be because they don't have to try as hard to get women there in the first place. But I'm just guessing about that.

3. Older does not mean wiser or more emotionally mature. Watch any middle-aged man trying to relive his youth with a red convertible and

chasing a twenty-something blonde
and you'll know exactly what I mean.

4.   You could put up a neon sign saying
'No!' and a man would still think
you're interested. Sometimes you will
need a restraining order to get rid of
them.

5.   You could put up a neon sign on the
airport tarmac saying 'Yes!' and ask
air traffic control to wave the man in,
but he still won't make a move.

6.   Sometimes you will lust after a man
even if you know you have nothing in
common and never will. He will never
be a long-term prospect.

7.   Sometimes a man will desperately
want to date you but it will be
abundantly clear that you have nothing
in common and never will.

8.   The laws of attraction frequently make
no sense. Don't analyse them and look
for meaning. There probably isn't any.

9.   Some men don't know what they want.
Others will work out what they want
much later, after you've left. You
could wait around until they make a
decision but, while you're distracted,

you could miss another great guy who's ready right now.

10. Complaining to a single, straight male friend about your single status might seem like a good idea but men will believe you're coming on to them even if you've said numerous times that your relationship is just platonic. Men can be bizarrely optimistic that way.

11. A real man will know what he wants and, if he wants you, he will make it very clear.

12. Sometimes, for some women, it really can be too small.

13. Sometimes it can be too big.

14. Five minutes of quality activity is preferable to 50 minutes of gratuitous banging against the headboard. Seriously, those nasal spray advertisements for erectile dysfunction have a lot to answer for!

15. Some men think good sex involves the woman being a passive participant. But if you wanted me to just lie there you should have purchased a blow-up doll from the nearest sex shop and taken it home with you.

16. Love can be an incredibly painful experience when it's not reciprocated.
17. You're never too old to have your heart broken.
18. Even when you think you know all the signs, sometimes the break-up will still surprise you.
19. Some women can forgive a man who cheats on them and live happily ever after. Some can't.
20. Just the thought of your current or former partner kissing another woman can make you vomit, literally.
21. In times of heartbreak and gut-wrenching sadness, it's amazing how often you will find yourself sobbing on the floor.
22. Married and otherwise attached men can be very persuasive. But it's wise to proceed with caution. Too often they've done it before and they'd do it again if they were attached to you.
23. Affairs happen and are often the result of recklessness and boredom. Just remember to use birth control because pregnancy can be a devastating consequence.

The Men I've Almost Dated

24. Never, ever put a new man above your friends. Ever.
25. If all your friends hate him, there's probably a good reason.
26. Any man who constantly lies, and borrows money from you and never pays it back, is a loser and should be deleted from your contact list. Permanently.
27. He should pay for your first date. After all, he asked you out. If he can't afford the meal then he shouldn't have taken you there. Better to have an ice cream date that he pays for than an impressive meal that you pay for. A good date doesn't have to be expensive.
28. Yes, he should open the door for you. It's not patronising; it's good manners.
29. Any man who yells at you when you're naked should be kicked out of your bed and out of your life.
30. Never stay with a man who hits you, abuses you verbally or tries to emotionally manipulate you. It's unlikely he'll change and you can do better.

Lucretia Ackfield

He Knows What He Wants, What He Really, Really Wants

A lot of women, including me, have made excuses for the less than ideal behaviour of our latest crush.

'Oh, he didn't realise what he was doing and didn't mean to lead me on' or 'He's lost my number' we'll say. There's also the classic, 'He's very shy and is scared of making the first move.' Then we'll make more excuses when he flees the scene like 'I didn't let him know strongly enough that I was interested' or 'I was too honest, too early in the relationship.'

Our list of excuses for shitty male behaviour goes on, and on and on. But these days my response to these statements is, 'What a load of crap!'

Men are grown-ups even if some of them don't always behave like it. They do the same things we do every morning - get dressed, leave the house, live their lives in the world, manage to feed themselves, have a social life and pay their bills.

Too often we talk about them as if they couldn't get by without us or they're not as responsible for their own behaviour. I am as guilty of this as every other woman out there who has suffered disappointment at the hands of a careless man and made excuses for it.

I'm not sure why we let ourselves believe this stuff.

When he said 'I'll call you' but I never heard from him again it meant, deaths and horrific accidents notwithstanding, he had something that was more important to do, wasn't interested or just wanted to find a way to end the conversation/date/meeting in a non-confrontational, non-hurtful way.

If he consistently forgets to call then it's better to just walk away. If I like someone, even just a platonic friend, I keep my commitments and turn up or call when I say I will. It's not brain surgery; it's courtesy.

Men, like us, can lose track of the time when they're out with friends, at a work function, visiting family and so on. But, if this means a desultory phone call more than

48 hours later then you need to seriously question if this is a considerate man who wants to get to know you or a deadbeat who can't be bothered putting you at the top of his priority list.

Likewise, if you consistently do not call or show up when you say you will, the man will think he's not important to you. He'll either try harder for your attention (because he'll believe you're playing hard to get) or start looking for company elsewhere.

Men are also capable of making up their minds about what they want. You may just need to give them some alone time to work it out. Once they make the decision they will do whatever it takes to attain that goal. They will call you, send an email or ask a mutual friend to set you up. They will find out what interests you and remember things you've previously said. They will want to know about you, what you think and how you feel.

Men who lead you on will also know what they are doing. For example, if he behaves like he's interested - flirting, unnecessary touching, looking meaningfully into your eyes – then he knows exactly what he's doing.

The Men I've Almost Dated

Of course, he might have liked you at the start and then his interest waned. But if he was never really interested or worse, if he was never available to start with, then he is responsible for his behaviour. He knows what he wants, what he really, really wants.[4]

---

[4] Variation on lyrics from the Spice Girls hit, *Wannabe* (1996).

Lucretia Ackfield

Reaching Relationship Man

I felt like I knew my partner when we were married. I developed a good understanding of how he thought and, through him, I gained insights into how his mates thought.

But when I found myself in break-up 'no man's land' I suddenly had absolutely no idea what the heck was going on. One minute I'd understood the male species but then all previous evidence and insight was gone. The rules I knew no longer applied. If I'd found myself on a singles game show, I would've answered every question incorrectly.

Men and women are always honest and up front about how they feel.

Brrgzz…Wrong!

A man will put you at the top of his priority list.

Brrgzz…wrong!

The Men I've Almost Dated

He'll make his feelings clear and you'll understand what's going on for him.

Brrgzz…wrong!

Men are reliable, and arrive and call when they say they will.

Brrgzz…wrong! Wrong! Wrong!

The truth is these qualities belong to a special man - Relationship Man. And I'll have to put in a lot of work and have a lot of luck before I see that type of man again. Relationship Man makes sense. You understand how he works. But any new partner will have a bucket load of experiences and emotional baggage just like me. Of course, I won't know about any of this when I meet him. Basically I'll have to go in unprepared without prior knowledge and slowly feel my way.

Even then I may not reach Relationship Man for months. And I know I can't rush it. It will happen in its own time and I'll just have to go with it. If I'm too full-on at the start I may inadvertently push that potential prince out the door.

I also need to leave my expectations, built on the backs of other partners in the past. I won't have a shared history with a new partner. So the minute I swing a bag full of expectations at his head, he's probably going to duck and run.

I'd love to say I'll be able to leave all my prior relationship experiences behind me and begin a new relationship with a shiny, fresh perspective. But I'm a realist. We all have expectations of what our relationships should be like.

The best thing I can do to reach Relationship Man again is give myself and the new man time for the dust to settle before I start talking about marriage, real estate and where to spend Christmas.

The 80/20 Rule

Sometimes we spend so much time trying to make our relationships work that we forget to check if we're actually happy or even in a relationship we want.

I spent a lot of time trying to make my marriage work even though my heart knew I didn't want to be there anymore. Over the years I've found myself repeating the same mistake by staying with or pursuing a man even when it's become destructive for my self-esteem or he's simply stopped returning my calls.

Now I try to live by the 80/20 rule. That's 80 percent good versus 20 percent bad.

If the relationship is the other way around, it's probably time to ask if I'm really helping myself to be happy. Staying in a relationship that is making me miserable, angry, frustrated or just plain dissatisfied most of the time is probably not the smartest thing I can do.

Lucretia Ackfield

More than once I've tried desperately to keep a relationship with a man even though I haven't been happy. He might have been appallingly unreliable, emotionally messed up, unavailable, inconsiderate or clearly not ready for a relationship but I kept trying to make it work. Even now I'm not sure why I did it.

These days I try to watch out for the early warning signs and exit gracefully. Being with the wrong person is worse than being alone. I'm also fed up with accepting crap behaviour, blaming myself or simply letting men off the hook. I don't care what his excuse is. I deserve the best.

I want a functioning and healthy relationship where the needs of both parties are met. I am not a doormat. So the 80/20 rule applies. If he makes me happy 80 per cent of the time - makes me feel good, cares about how I feel, makes time to have fun with me and so on then I'm in. Otherwise, I'll pull the plug.

In the words of my very wise friend Janine, 'Sometimes Lucretia, you just have to kick them to the curb.'

The Men I've Almost Dated

What Was I Thinking?

I've made a few unwise decisions when it comes to men. Okay. I've made a lot of really dumb, ill-informed and naïve decisions when it comes to men. I've done things I never thought I would do, like have an affair with an older, overweight, balding tradesman who couldn't get it up. I've also embarked on a few short-lived romances with men who are far too young to be sensible and fancied myself in love with some of them.

These are some of the tamer examples.

Among all these adventures, there have been a few moments when I've bumped into one of my paramours several months or years later and thought, 'OH MY GOD! What was I thinking?'

I realise that if I'd been a little saner, more rational, or less drunk, emotionally bereft, desperate or horny those men would never have made it into my life and I would have never been interested in ripping their clothes off with my teeth.

Hindsight always shines a spotlight on the obviousness of it all. But I have done my best to forgive myself for my crazier decisions. My exes, however short-term, simply represent another less evolved part of my history and it's probably best if I leave it that way…in the past. It's better to take the lessons I've learned and yes, perhaps relish the naughtiness of it all, feel blessed that I came through it all relatively unscathed, and keep moving forward.

I might also need to change my number so that tradesman stops calling.

When I first wrote about some of my more cringe-worthy single experiences in my blog, lucyandlife.com, I had an amazing response. It seemed a lot of women could relate to those things in my past that I'd rather forget but somehow, never will.

The Men I've Almost Dated

So here is a list of the stupid stuff I've done, or thought about doing, as a single woman. It's a bit embarrassing but I'm pretty sure you'll have your own list as well.

1. Dated a man half my age and considered moving towns to be closer to him. He lived out west and in the end I decided, 'You can't wear stilettoes in the dirt,' so I stayed in the city.
2. Had a fling with my sister's ex-boyfriend. My sister dated him more than a decade earlier and said she was fine with it. But I don't think Dad liked it. Apparently when Mum broke the news he said, 'Do you mean Paul has had sex with two of my daughters!?!' Sorry Dad.
3. Had a fling with my housemate. He moved out and I didn't have anyone to help with the bills. I never did ask him for his share of the electricity bill either.
4. Assumed that a man was single when he consistently flirted with me and acted like he was unattached. I should have asked early on, 'Do you have a girlfriend/wife?' It would have saved

me a lot of pain and disappointment,
several times.

5. Fallen in love with the wrong men and
    had my heart repeatedly broken or
    seriously dented.

6. Naïvely believed that a married man
    would never proposition me when his
    wife was only metres away.

7. Continued to date a man when the sex
    was atrocious from the start. Seriously,
    if it doesn't improve after a couple of
    times, there's probably a good reason
    and it may be you're just not
    compatible.

8. Blamed myself when a man couldn't get
    it up in the bedroom.

9. Tried to start something new with a man
    who has just come out of a long-term
    relationship. I seem to attract these men
    a lot and it never works out well for me.

10. Became emotionally involved with a
    man too quickly. Having sex with them
    too soon only makes this worse.

11. Made a pass at my boss because I was
    bored and wanted to see what he'd do.

12. Obsessed about an unattainable man for
    years and seriously considered putting

notes on the windscreen of his car to tell him how I felt.

13. Assumed that everyone is comfortable with honesty, particularly men.

14. Been way too open about how I feel. This is a turn-off for some men, apparently.

15. Assumed a man is going to ask me out because he obviously likes being in my personal space, compliments me a lot and gets annoyed when other men flirt with me.

16. Sent letters to men telling them how wonderful I think they are and how they've made me feel, after they've broken up with me. Writing things down always makes me feel better but I really need to write the letter and burn it. Note to self, DO NOT SEND IT!

17. Sent a card to my flirtatious doctor that included my name, mobile number and the words, 'Because life is too short'.

18. Flirted with another male doctor so much that he left the door open during our consultation.

19. Allowed myself to be attracted to men who have demonstrated 'lame' qualities

Lucretia Ackfield

that I repeatedly ignored. By 'lame' I mean any of the warning signs that an impartial person would interpret as code for 'run like hell away from this man immediately'.

The Men I've Almost Dated

Don't Give Up Your Life For A Man

While I was married I studied, went out
with friends and had interests that were
separate from my husband. Daniel also did
some of his own things like football, squash
and car-related activities. This meant the
times we spent together were more
meaningful because we had different things
and experiences to share with each other.

As a single girl I've continued my extra-
curricular activities and some weeks I'll be
out most nights doing various activities or
catching up with friends.

I'd rather be out, keeping fit,
volunteering, meeting people and
experiencing new things than staying in,
watching television and feeling sorry for
myself (although I sometimes do that as
well). However, I do have some single
girlfriends who feel that going out on a
school night is almost revolutionary. My
busy life seems a little unusual to them.
Tara's reasoning for this became clear when

Lucretia Ackfield

I mentioned I wanted to sit on the board of a not-for-profit organisation. This would be in addition to my recent gym membership, two dance classes a week and volunteering.

If a friend had announced a similar plan my response would have been, 'Is that hard to do?' and 'That sounds like a great idea.' But Tara's response was a little different.

'What will you give up if you meet someone though? I mean you won't be able to do all that as well,' she said. For a moment I was speechless.

'If I meet someone, the right man, he will fit in around what's already in my life just as I'll fit in around his. If he can't then he's not the man for me,' I said. And that, as far as I was concerned, was that.

I was appalled Tara thought she needed to restrict herself and give up something when she met a man. She believed she'd have to move her life around to accommodate a new partner. The man wasn't even on the scene yet but he was already restricting her movements.

Choosing not to do something because a man might be around the corner seems a little crazy to me. What if he never shows up?

I also believe that a man will like me more because I have a life of my own. Most men don't want a woman who is co-dependent and smothering him with neediness. Do they?

I am interested in meeting a 'real man' - not some namby pampy human with no sense of self who needs to be with me all the time; not some control freak who wants me to be co-dependent so he can watch me every minute. A. Real. Man.

I also don't want someone who arranges his life completely around me and has no interests unless they fit exactly in with mine. Quite frankly, I would prefer a fully-grown adult who likes me having a life of my own.

Lucretia Ackfield

The Unassailable Truth: Perfection Does Not Exist

In my search for a partner I have learned one unassailable truth, there is no such thing as a perfect relationship. Even soul mates bicker when one of them washes the red towel with the white shirts.

Perhaps the truly amazing thing is that any of us ever form a long-term relationship at all. We are so different, every single one of us. We all want to go our own way and do our own thing. So I don't look for perfection in a partner as it doesn't exist. Instead I think it's far wiser to aim for a partner who has imperfections that I can live with and love.

A lot of women worry about their imperfections. We wonder if our breasts, backsides, stomachs and other parts are too big or too small. The truth is that men are the same. They worry about these things too.

So when one asked me proudly, 'Does my dick look bigger now?' because he'd shaved his pubic hair, my very appropriate response was, 'Of course'.

The conversation also explained why there was a lot of curly hair on the bathmat.

Lucretia Ackfield

The Single Advantage

Being single can be lonely one day and liberating the next. I have definitely missed having a partner at times. But on other occasions, after observing yet another dysfunctional relationship, I've yelled a secret 'Hurrah for no men!' on the inside.

There are a few things I haven't missed while being single.
1. The Pill (and the associated weight gain).
2. A man peeing in my toilet with the door open.
3. The seat always being left up on the toilet no matter how many times I politely ask a man to PUT IT DOWN!
4. Co-ordinating my social arrangements around the football, swimming, motor racing or other sporting events.

The Men I've Almost Dated

On the downside, I have missed a few things too.

1. Someone holding me.
2. Sex. I could find a 'friend with benefits' or simply pick someone up and take them home for casual entertainment. But that doesn't compare to the intimacy of having sex with a long-term partner who regularly shares my bed.
3. Romantic getaways. I am so sick of hearing friends talk about romantic weekends away in cabins with fireplaces, champagne and chocolates. I know I could book one with a friend but, as I'm not a lesbian, it would be kind of weird.
4. Sharing life decisions. Sometimes it would be nice to be able to turn to a partner and say, 'What do you think sweetheart? Should we go to Italy or Greece? or 'Do you think we should renovate the house or move?' or 'Do you think moving interstate for that job is a good idea?' I'm not looking for a man's permission to do something but it would be nice to discuss these things with a life-partner.

I've also discovered there are a lot of advantages to the single life. Here are some of my favourites.

1. I don't have to listen to someone snoring. I might snore but I'll already be asleep so who cares.
2. I can see whatever movie I want, when I want. I also don't have to hear my partner sighing and muttering under his breath, 'I don't see what's so great about movies with subtitles. Can't they just do an English version?'
3. I don't have to worry about my date/husband/partner falling asleep during the most dramatic part of the latest theatre production. Daniel once managed to doze off during a very convincing rape scene. I still don't know how that was possible.
4. I don't have to feign interest as my partner's boring best mate talks endlessly at every social occasion about his latest passion and hobby. Trust me, it will be a sport and I am just being polite. I don't really care about baiting hooks, football or Tiger Woods' swing.

The Men I've Almost Dated

5. I can sit in almost any row at the movies even if I arrive late and the room is packed. There is always a single seat in one of the best rows in the house.

6. There is only one person to consider when I plan my next travelling adventure – me (and my cat).

7. I can spend my holidays wherever I want. I don't have to say, 'Sure, I guess I could give camping a go this Easter' even when I'd prefer a proper bed and my own bathroom.

8. I don't have to check in with someone else when I decide to go overseas on short notice.

9. I don't have to accommodate someone else's bad taste in furniture in my home. Is it really compulsory that comfortable chairs must also be incredibly ugly?

10. I can spend holidays with whoever I want - not my partner's permanently red-nosed Great Uncle Jack who drinks like a fish and will probably knock over my fence with his car as he exits the driveway.

11. I am not repeatedly cajoled into spending Friday, Saturday and Sunday nights at home because the football is on.

12. I don't have to be nice to someone who steals the blankets or complains the room is too hot.

13. I don't have to freeze my arse off in the car because someone else needs the air conditioning set at 19 degrees. This goes for motel rooms as well.

14. I don't have to lose my temper, silently shred my own tongue or abruptly leave the table because a member of someone else's family thinks racist, sexist or other discriminatory remarks are appropriate in the modern world. Nor do I have to calmly inform them that ambulance chasing reporters from one of the 'high-quality' current affairs programs are not experts on all events.

15. I can eat whatever I want, when I want. I never have to tolerate someone who raises an eyebrow and says something like, 'Should you be eating that?' or 'You're getting a bit heavy you know.' (Fortunately I've never been with a man

who tried this behaviour with me but if one ever does, I'll be slamming my cream bun into his face.)

16. I don't have to listen to someone telling me that they'd prefer I change out of the clothes I've selected and wear a different outfit that is more revealing, less revealing or simply more to his taste. (As per the previous example, this has occurred to friends but not me. Men who try this approach may be kicked in a very sensitive part of their anatomy.)

17. I don't have to listen to someone tell me that I'd fill out my top even better AND improve my self-esteem if I got a boob job. (Seriously, when I hear my girlfriends tell these stories I wonder if anyone has suggested these men get a penis enhancement or surgery to remove the extra dick that's protruding from their forehead.)

18. I don't have to sit across from someone else and think, 'Why do they insist on wearing board shorts when it is less than 15 degrees?' or 'The person who invented Crocs should be shot!'

19. I can keep my car and house as messy or clean as I like.
20. I don't have to wonder why someone doesn't call, is late and hasn't called, or doesn't show up and doesn't call.
21. I don't have to pretend that sure, of course I don't mind being woken up at 5am every day because you start work early or feel the need to exercise at the crack of dawn.

There are very few moments when you feel completely free and in charge of your life and your destiny. When you're single, these can occur when you're driving your car, you don't have to be anywhere and no one is expecting you. Your time is exclusively your own. It's an amazing feeling.

Don't Break the Deal Breakers

I slowed down my car the other day to let a four-wheel-drive utility merge into traffic. The driver was a construction worker who looked like he'd just finished his shift and was heading home.

I caught a glimpse of his face and thought, 'Hello!' He had those rugged Australian good looks often associated with tradesmen. When he lifted a hand off the window frame and smiled his thanks I thought 'Hello!' times two. He was definitely very, very attractive.

Then it went downhill.

As we waited for the cars to move he took off his shirt to reveal arms full of tattoos. Then he lit a cigarette and hung his arm out the window. Those three small things were enough to break the spell for me and the attraction was gone.

The combination of the all-over tattoos, the cigarette drooping from the corner of his mouth and hanging his arm out the car like a yobo was a deal breaker for me.

Every woman has deal breakers or things that turn them off a man no matter how nice he is. Sometimes they can seem completely rational and logical to other people. Other times you might think that someone's deal breakers are completely insane.

They can reflect our value systems, what we believe is important and how we want to live our lives and treat others. They may also be the result of situations we've seen while growing up, how our parents treated each other, how we've seen our friends treated or our previous relationship experiences.

When I've compromised on my deal breakers, it hasn't ended well. For example, I have a 'no illegal drugs' rule because I've seen how they can destroy people. I have friends who take recreational drugs and as far as I'm concerned, that's their business. But if I'm sleeping with you, then it's not on. I can't invest my time, my trust and my heart in someone who'd prefer to get high than experience life in a more conscious state. I simply believe that prolonged drug use will fry your beautiful brain and eventually steal your soul; I need my partner to be whole and present.

A few years ago I found myself in a relationship with a guy called John who said he'd stopped using recreational drugs before we met. I knew he had a history with drugs but I chose to believe they were in his past. I do, after all, believe anyone can change if they choose to.

A couple of months later, he told me he'd slipped and smoked pot. To a lot of people it would be no big deal. But John knew my no-drugs rule and I was devastated. Even as I forgave him, I knew I was going in the wrong direction. I was compromising myself because by that stage, I was in love with him.

What followed was every bit of dysfunction you could possibly fit into a relationship. He lied, did drugs (more pot, speed and who knows what else), was manipulative, cruel, hung around with known criminals and in the end, cheated on me.

He was the 'bad boy' I skipped when I was in my 20s.

If I'd just been true to my deal breaker, I could have escaped that relationship much earlier with a little more dignity and lot less emotional devastation. Lesson learned.

Deal breakers are different for everyone. One friend ended a relationship with a guy because his hands were too big. My friend Simon was incredibly offended when he heard that story – and his hands weren't large.

A short survey of my friends revealed deal breakers that were diverse and hilarious.

KERRY: I dumped a guy once because he had a mole on the end of his nose. Not a moley person in general but I just found I couldn't look him in the eye.

MEGAN: STD's, mental health issues, addictions of any kind…steroid users, vanity, guys looking over my shoulder for something better, missing the toilet and leaving urine drops on my floor…Did I mention std's? Herpes, genital warts…Can. Not. Go. There.

SELINA: Hmmmm cause he was short and had small hands!

The Men I've Almost Dated

KAITLIN: Making less money than me. Super skinny men! Guys who are not over their ex wives! Sexist men.

TERRI: Wouldn't date men with longer hair than me, skinnier than me or more feminine than me. Oh and that use the word 'crankin' in place of the word 'cool'.

LYNDA: When he says to me "Breast implants could improve your confidence".

JO: Men who are not over their exes!!!

AMANDA: My turnoff used to be when blokes pants were either too long or too short to sit nicely on their shoes...watch this one ladies as this shows a definite lack of class!!

ABBY: A man with more skin care products than me – the application of lip balm, particularly shiny lip balm (outside of an arctic zone or for sun protection) is an immediate offence. On the other extreme, men who can't form a sentence without using the "F" word as a joining word.

MIA: ...a man who shows up in a a truck with roo-shooting lights and a buffalo winch...

CASSIE: Or false advertising...Big men with small penises, or worse, small bendy penises. Thank god I broke up with him!!!

ELI: Being shorter than me!

SIMONE: ...their teeth – I'm okay with imperfect teeth, but if they can't manage to regularly brush their teeth that means (to me) they don't care about the whole personal hygiene thing...and I don't need or want to look any further.

TARA: Cannot date a bald man...And shaved heads get me nervous as you don't know if they are shaving on purpose.

LAUREN: Cannot even consider a blondie. Blondes just remind me of boys...If you want a man go brunette! And I refuse to colour his hair.

ROBIN: The usual...Teeth...I'm extremely picky...As most of us are. There is this absolutely gorgeous guy in the salon! So, so sexy...And he has a grey tooth. ☹

While the survey responses had me laughing aloud, they also confirmed one thing. We all have deal breakers and they can seem completely frivolous to someone else even when they are really important to

The Men I've Almost Dated

you. But, based on my personal experience, breaking a deal breaker can almost break you.

Old Man Fear

When things haven't been going well dating-wise, it can be hard to recognise when things might actually be going my way. Sometimes I've almost given up and started believing I am the reason men don't stay around. I've even sabotaged relationships before they could start.

I've put up emotional walls and shut down every guy who makes a pass at me. I've been so terrified of rejection that I've retreated and instead of flashing a smile and flirting up a storm I've hidden with my friends in a corner. And I'm an extrovert!

I've also gone to the other extreme and acted like a needy fruitcake after only two dates. I was terrified of rejection and being hurt again. So my solution was to have an emotional meltdown. In that situation, fear was in control and destroying the opportunity that was right in front of me.

Other times I've realised a man is interested hours or sometimes days after the moment has passed. I've been so blinded by my disillusionment and insecurities that I completely missed the signs. It's a bad habit I started in high school.

I had a crush on Jeremy when I was 16-years-old. I thought there was no way he'd ever be interested in me and I was too scared to reveal that I liked him. So he'd smile at me and I'd smile back. Then I'd walk briskly in the opposite direction. One day, one of my hair combs fell out and dropped into the school grate near the library. Jeremy eagerly offered to retrieve it for me. I wanted the comb back (it was purple and very stylish in the 80s) but I was too self-conscious to accept his help. So I pretended it didn't matter and virtually ran away.

Years later, long after high school had ended, I bumped into Jeremy at the local shopping center. He confessed he'd had the biggest crush on me at exactly the same time as I'd liked him. We laughed and moved on but I wondered what would've happened if I'd just put aside my fear and believed that someone I liked could like me back.

I always visualise my fear as an old cranky and disillusioned old man who crouches on my shoulder, sulks and whispers words of doubt and discouragement into my ear.

'No, you can't do that because you're single and everyone else will be there in couples,' he'll say.

'You can't just turn up at that event or new restaurant by yourself. You can't go on your own. Everyone will think you're pathetic,' he'll advise.

You can see he's not the supportive type.

The first time I went to the movies alone I initially felt like a complete loser. Old Man Fear whispered in my ear that everyone was looking at me and thinking, 'How sad and lonely she must be'. But still I persevered.

Once the previews started, my fear and self-consciousness evaporated. Old Man Fear disappeared. As a single person I could sit anywhere I wanted and didn't have to worry if the person next to me was enjoying or hating the movie. The box of Malteasers was also all mine. It was a liberating experience.

It seems crazy now that I was so concerned about what other people might be thinking about me. In hindsight, it's unlikely

The Men I've Almost Dated

that anyone noticed me at all. Nowadays, I try to regulate my interaction with Old Man Fear. I've also gained the perspective to see him for what he is – a collection of insecurities and self-judgement that can restrict my life and reduce my chances for happiness. I also don't worry so much about what people think and rejection isn't as scary as it used to be. If a man does reject me I will still get up the next morning, a little older and wiser perhaps, but still alive with a future full of unexpected surprises, love and happiness. I just have to believe in it, and in myself.

Lucretia Ackfield

Demolish the Comfort Zone

'I'm finally remembering what it is to have control of my life again. My choices, my plans, my consequences.

I'd almost lost that part of myself – she'd become hidden behind a screen of insecurities and doubt. But now, POW, she's back baby! She's back.'

I wrote these words in a journal while I sat in Munich Airport in August 2010, slowly spooning hot chocolate into my mouth, grinning like a crazy person and feeling just so grateful to be alive, single and unencumbered by anyone or anything.

But a week earlier, as I planned my trip, I was filled with panic.

I hadn't travelled overseas for two years and my life was shambolic and emotionally turbulent. My confidence was down and my mind swam in the blackness of doubt. I wasn't sure if I was still brave enough to travel on my own.

The Men I've Almost Dated

My friend Tyler had been full of
encouragement and shared a few wise words
before I left. I'd confided that the recent
chaos in my life made me want to stay in my
comfort zone. 'Yeah, but once you get out of
your comfort zone you will more than likely
fall into another one but with different
dimensions...I guess that's how people
grow,' he said.

Even now those words choke me up.
They said so much about how we sometimes
live or run from our lives because we're too
scared to step away from what we know
towards what could be.

When you're single and you've had some
bad experiences, it's really easy to get
sucked into that zone and stay there. But
when that happens, you'll find yourself
doing the same things you've always done,
seeing what you've always seen and meeting
the same types of people everywhere you
go.

As for that melancholic longing you'll
feel for the last relationship where you felt
comfortable - if you were truly happy with
that last person you'd still be with them,
doing all the things you used to do, eating at

the places you used to go and sleeping on the same side of the bed you've always slept in. So maybe that comfortable relationship wasn't actually so great after all.

I've realised that while the comfort zone is good for a while, it also confines me to a small box while the rest of the world waits right outside. So I try to bust out of the box occasionally. I'll do something I've never done before; something I've been too scared to try. I'll just do it! And it will be for myself and not to make another person happy. It might be a class I've always wanted to take, a volunteer role I'm interested in or I might go to a Meet-up where I will know no-one else in the room.

Once I do that thing, whatever it is, I'll feel a little stronger than I did yesterday, a little more confident than I felt last week, and a lot more comfortable with the fact that I am on my own and can kick arse!

Every time that feeling starts to fade, I throw myself out of my comfort zone again. Sometimes I have to force myself. I may have to prise my fingers from whatever they are holding on to – how things used to be, who I was, or that old boyfriend or husband.

The Men I've Almost Dated

For me, getting out of my comfort zone has often involved jumping on a plane and going overseas. I rarely travel with company and there are always a few doubters.

'You be very careful,' they'll say. 'Are you sure it's safe?' Their tone will suggest I'm being foolhardy.

'I could never travel by myself,' one man said to me like I was doing something brave (and this was a fireman who ran into burning buildings for a living!).

But I don't listen. Instead I trust my gut and do what I need to do, for me. Is that brave? I don't really think so. I've just realised that life is too short to stay static for too long. Besides, I could meet someone interesting on the plane or in that cooking class. I might meet the love of my life or stumble into a new life altogether.

I think some women stay in their comfort zone because we don't like to do things alone. We like to do things in couples. We'd like to travel, go to the movies, renovate our house and have children with someone by our side.

But here's a revolutionary idea. Go it alone. Don't be afraid because the world is full of women who are going solo every day. They're doing a great job and having fun.

I'm not saying we should make men redundant in our lives. They are way too much fun to abandon altogether. I'm just suggesting that going it alone will help ensure you don't miss out on any experience because you're waiting for Mr Right to knock on your door.

Make your own plans, for you. You don't have to accommodate anyone else's views. You can even paint your own walls purple with pink polka dots if you want to – it's your house.

And if you really want children and your time is running out, make your plans now. It won't be easy but you know what, you might meet your dream man at 55 and his sperm will be no use to you because the biological door will have slammed shut.

After all, would you put your career on hold while you waited for that perfect man to walk through your door? I don't think so. The rest of your life should be no different.

The Men I've Almost Dated

Break-ups Won't Kill You

I'm sure some women handle break-ups in a very healthy, constructive and grown up way. They probably become very Zen-like and take only the lessons of the relationship before moving calmly into their future. They don't try to hang onto the man who left them. They don't obsess about what he's doing. They don't stalk him anonymously on Facebook. And they certainly don't feel depressed, cry a lot or fantasise about running their cheating ex-boyfriend over with their car.

Unfortunately, I am not one of those Zen-like women. I don't respond well to break-ups and I often feel very old after some careless man breaks my heart. I don't mean old like a 90-year-old with creaking bones and a walking stick (although sometimes a stick would be great to beat certain men over the head with). I mean old like the life has mostly left my body, leaving it so brittle it is almost transparent and crumbling around the edges. Just weeks or days earlier I would be overflowing with life, bursting at the seams with joy, then suddenly it's all gone.

Break-ups are invariably painful because relationships rarely end amicably and mutually. One person always wants to move on before the other is quite ready. You might smile and say, 'Of course, I agree. Yes, I know it's obvious that we're not really suited for a long-term relationship.'

But you'll be lying.

In most of my relationships, the man has broken up with me. I've been the 'dumpee' and have experienced a range of feelings, thoughts and reactions during break-ups.

Peter dumped me over lunch and I had two reasons to feel angry afterwards. I was upset when he told me it was over but when I became visibly distressed he sharply admonished me like I was a small child and said, 'It's nothing to get upset about'. He also let me pay for his lunch.

Anthony came to my house, cooked me dinner and said 'I haven't opened up to anyone like this in years'. An hour later he said, 'I have to break-up with you or I'll break your heart'. My thoughts were,

The Men I've Almost Dated

'Breaking up with me is going to break my heart.'

He followed this with, 'Better to end it now than have a train wreck later.' I guess me sitting on the floor sobbing didn't qualify as a train wreck to him.

Just to stick the knife in completely, the reason he broke up with me was my no-drugs policy. He'd rather smoke pot than be with me. What a charmer.

I'm pretty sure he'd decided to break-up with me before he came to my house that night. Now I wondered why he bothered to show up at all.

Lucretia Ackfield

What I Should Have Said

The words spoken at the end of a relationship can haunt you for days, weeks, months or years. Often they are complete rubbish because men rarely have the guts to tell the truth. They just want to get the hell out of there and away from me as quickly as possible. They don't want to feel bad about themselves for long.

Here are some of the worst break-up lines ever spoken and what I wished I'd said in response.

'I want someone I can take care of.'

Someone needs to give this guy a lesson in relationship dynamics. 'Do you want a partner or a baby?!'

*

'I can't love you the way you want to be loved.'

I still can't think of an appropriate response to this one because it's just so stupid.

The Men I've Almost Dated

*

'It's not you, it's me.'

Yes, men are still saying this. If you ever hear this one I recommend the following response, 'Yes it is you, you moron and by the way, can't you think of something original!'

*

'You taught me about love. I thought I knew what it was before I met you, but I realised that I didn't.'

Thanks pal. 'Did you think about that when you were having sex with the backpacker you picked up at the local pub on the same day you had phone sex with me?'

*

'I'm really messed up right now, I just need to find out who I am before I can be any use to someone else.'

'Couldn't you have told me that before you slept with me three times and I introduced you to everyone at my birthday party last week? And by the way, my best friend thought you were a wanker, but she didn't have the heart to tell me.'

Lucretia Ackfield

*

'I just can't do this anymore.'

Unfortunately, this is one of the most honest break-up lines. It may hurt and twist the knife in your heart, but it cannot be refuted or mocked.

Most of us really do see the break-up asteroid before it slams into our chest and splits us apart. There are always signs. Sometimes they're obvious, sometimes they're subtle, but they are always there.

Here are some of the signs I've witnessed.

1. He starts to pull away ever so slightly. I'll be half way through a sentence and suddenly he'll be talking about a completely different subject as if he wasn't listening to me at all.

2. He won't ask me questions about my day or what I think. The conversation doesn't bubble merrily, it kind of gurgles near a drain. I'll wonder why he's gone quiet but I'll assume he's just gone into the 'man cave' to think for a while, so I'll give him space.

The Men I've Almost Dated

3. Seeing me naked appears to be a little less interesting than it was previously. Hugging and just hanging out becomes the preferred option.
4. He turns away from me to sleep. Everything might seem fine, the sex will be great but then I'll be presented with his back and he'll doze off. It's such a subtle thing but it's always resulted in the same outcome.
5. He'll start using the 'too' word about me. 'You're too melodramatic, too sexual, to over the top, too emotional, too affectionate, too...you.'

Did I mention that I hate break-ups?

Lucretia Ackfield

Heartbreak Recovery

I've used some or all of the following strategies to help me through break-ups. Some are a little unimaginative but they still work.

1. Have a good cry while sitting on the floor. Inevitably, in times of great anguish, it seems natural to be as close to the ground as possible. When ready, you can progress to sobbing in the foetal position on your bed and later, sobbing while sitting on the couch watching chick flicks.

2. Spoon large amounts of chocolate ice-cream plus chocolate sauce and cream (if you have it) into an extremely large bowl (feel free to use the ice-cream container for this), put *Bridget Jones's Diary* into the DVD player and ensure tissues are nearby. Follow this with DVDs such as *Bridget Jones: Age of Reason*, any romantic comedy featuring

The Men I've Almost Dated

Meg Ryan, *Dirty Dancing* and the BBC version of *Pride and Prejudice*. Repeat this step as required.

3. Try to leave the house occasionally and exercise. It is harder to feel depressed when you're in the sunlight. However, seeing couples holding hands and stepping in unison can push your recovery back a little. Fill your pockets with tissues just in case.

4. Listen to empowering songs. My current favourites are *Wide Awake* (Katy Perry) and *Undefeated* (Jason Derulo). If you're feeling really dark (and perhaps a little angry) basically anything from *Jagged Little Pill* (Alanis Morissette) works well.

5. Make a list of the all the things that annoyed you about [insert his name here]. You'll be surprised how many you can come up with. This is a great exercise because it forces you to acknowledge there were things you didn't like. No one is perfect. He definitely isn't perfect. DO NOT send him the list. I repeat, DO NOT send him the list no matter how drunk you are.

6. Write [insert his name here] a letter
    telling him how you feel but DO NOT
    SEND IT TO HIM. Shred the letter,
    burn it or flush it down the toilet. You
    may need to write this letter several
    times to purge him from your system.
7. Try to ignore that little spark of hope in
    your heart. You know the spark I'm
    talking about. It's that naïve hope he
    will realise what a stupid decision he's
    made and will rush through your door
    any moment, sweep you into his arms
    and it will all work out.
8. Don't be the 'nice' girl and say, 'Sure I
    can stay in touch and be just friends,'
    because YOU CAN'T! You're not
    impartial, even if he is. He has basically
    stabbed you in the heart and you need
    recovery time. Think of it as if you've
    had heart surgery - no one would expect
    you to run a marathon the next day. You
    may be 'just friends' later but you can't
    do it right now. Besides he'll find it
    hard to be friends with someone who
    wants to alternately kiss him, have sex

with him or punch him in the nose. You will want to do all those things.

9. Hang out with your wonderful girlfriends. They will give you hugs, listen to your break-up story (repeatedly), tell you how fabulous you are and say that he is not worth your tears because he walked (or ran) away.

10. You may have thought [his name] was wonderful, but he left. Maybe it was a timing thing or maybe there is someone far more fabulous around the corner. Trust that fate has better plans for you. Look forward, not back and know you'll be okay. Eventually.

*

There are lots of sensible things you can do when a man breaks up with you.

When you keep the text messages, photos and things he gave you, he is still going to be present in your life. If you're like me, you'll go back and re-read messages, cry over photos of the two of you together and the gifts he gave you. The things he left behind, his toothbrush, his bottle of tequila and shot glasses, or that DVD will mock you.

You need to remove the evidence.

Delete his text messages. You probably won't be able to do this for a while but it will definitely help you to not dwell on the things you shared. If you don't feel strong enough to throw his things out or give them away, hide them in the back of a cupboard somewhere. Seeing them every day will only upset you.

I once took this approach a little too far. Brent and I had just called it off (it was sort of mutual but still very painful). So there I was manically stripping sheets from the bed (where we'd just had sex) while simultaneously yelling down the hallway, 'Don't forget your DVD!'

He walked back up the hallway in time to see me ripping the last of the bedding from the mattress and said, 'You're trying to get rid of the evidence that I was here, aren't you?'

'Yes,' I said.

'Thought so.' He knew exactly what I was trying to do. It was just a shame his understanding of how my mind worked didn't translate into him wanting to date me long-term.

The Men I've Almost Dated

De-friending your ex on Facebook may seem a bit radical. After all, surely just hiding his news feed will stop you seeing his posts about partying with a blonde at the hottest club in town. But hiding his news feed won't be enough. You'll still be able to visit his page to find out what he's doing. You will go to his page repeatedly. You may even tell yourself that you're just checking his page to prove you don't feel anything for him anymore. You'll be lying.

The only way to break this cycle is to de-friend him. One press of a button is all it takes. So do it. On a personal note, this strategy would have been a lot more effective if Brent, for example, had full privacy settings enabled on his Facebook page. But he didn't so I could still obsessively check his status several times a day and sit staring at his photo wondering why he left and if I would ever recover. He really should be more careful because there are a lot of crackpots out there who could be cyberstalking him...like me.

It will also be tempting to visit the places your ex hangs out. If you bump into each other casually, he might realise what a terrible decision he's made and want you back. Or you might make yourself look completely desperate.

I recommend the absence makes the heart grow fonder approach. If he can't see or talk to you then he may start wondering what he's missing. If he doesn't wonder what you're doing, and he doesn't come and find you, then you need to move on. Try and hold onto what remains of your pride ladies. Desperation is never sexy.

The Goodbye Note

Writing a letter to an ex is a good way to say goodbye to an old relationship. Therapists, counselors and friends will often tell you to use letter writing to get that man out of your system. 'It will help you move on, you'll work through the issues and it will be easier to let go and deal with the pain,' they'll say wisely.

So we'll write the letter and it will feel good to express all that emotion welling up in our broken heart. And then, if you're like me, you'll send it. No one ever tells me to send these letters. In fact, most people have told me quite explicitly not to send them. Do. Not. Send. The. Letter.

Wise people will say, 'Don't let him know how much he's hurt you. It's none of his business now. He doesn't really care.' But have I listened to this wise advice? Sadly, no.

Instead I have posted that letter, hit send on that email or text and it was done. Then

just as the letter fluttered to the bottom of
the red post box or the icon disappeared
from my computer or phone screen, doubt
has set in.

What. Have. I. Done.

On one occasion, I received no reply to
the letter of pain and longing I sent to Jerry
but when I bumped into him a month later I
felt completely exposed and very foolish.

It's even worse when a man responds to
my letter, email or text because he's still
trying to be nice even though he doesn't
want me anymore. He probably just feels
kind of sorry for me.

I've foolishly sent many post-break-up
messages via various mediums. In one
foolish act, I sent the following text message
to an ex telling him how I felt:

*Brent, it's unkind of you to call me things
like sweetie and good looking when u don't
mean them. You broke my heart…remember.
And although I still care I am not a doormat
or stupid (although perhaps some people
might say when it comes to you I have been
both these things). We r not just mates and I
can't just act like nothing ever happened –
that would no doubt make you feel better but*

The Men I've Almost Dated

*i would feel lousy. Besides, in hindsight i
have realised there were many things about
me that made u uncomfortable so I don't
know why u would want to be mates w me
anyway. I am not over it and I do not have
the stomach to pretend I am. If at some point
u want to talk to me, u should probably do
that. I would (perhaps foolishly) still be
willing to hear what u have to say.*

Brent's response*: Wow that was a really
big text message.* ☺

Oh the humiliation.

I was still giving him a chance; still
letting him know the door was open if he
wanted to waltz back into my life. Clearly
my self-respect and feelings of self-worth
had taken a holiday.

I'm pretty sure I'm not alone in this type
of behaviour and I blame that little voice in
the back of our heads that whispers, 'If he
only knew how much you care about him
and see all his wonderful qualities then
he would realise what a terrible mistake
he's made.'

But the next time I hear that hopeful little
voice I will imagine I can hear that buzzer
from the old game shows when the

contestant got an answer wrong. And if that voice says, 'I just want him to know how much he hurt me,' I will listen for the sound of a large church bell being rung, deafeningly, in my right ear.

I'm going to imagine this because it's the truth. He really doesn't care enough. There, I've said it. Now I need to believe it. If he's dumped me, he doesn't care enough to be with me. Yes, I know in some rare cases a man will realise his mistake and come running back. But, if he does he will need to do it on his own and not because I send him 'please come back' letters.

The truth is, in 99.9 percent of cases, the man doesn't care anymore. Oh, he'll feel uncomfortable because he's probably a 'fairly' decent man who doesn't enjoy hurting other people. So he'll feel bad for a while and then he'll move on. If I send the letter he will probably read it, think about it for a few minutes and feel a little uncomfortable before sitting down to watch the cricket and forgetting all about it.

But, if I send multiple messages he might start looking over his shoulder and worrying that I'm a stalker. Please keep this in mind if

The Men I've Almost Dated

a man cheated on you and the break-up was acrimonious. Letters that include the phrases, 'If I see you on the footpath I'll run you down' or 'I want to remove your balls with a carving knife' may lead to police officers arriving on your doorstep.

However, it's difficult to just write letters and not do anything with them. Here are some of my disposal methods.

1. Tear it up into little pieces and flush it down the toilet. This approach is only recommended if your letter is one or two pages long. Any longer and you'll have to explain yourself to the local plumber. Then again, if he's cute and single, go for it.

2. Put the letter into a fireproof container in an open space outside and light it up. A match will do the job easily so please don't use inflammable liquid - a newly single girl really does need her eyebrows intact. If you feel the need to dance around, swear or cry hysterically as the last of the embers burn then by all means do so. Just make it a good show because the neighbour's are probably watching.

3. Screw up the letter and throw it in the nearest bin. This is not as dramatic or cathartic and, unless your bin is being collected that night, you may feel the letter taunting you the next day.
4. Take the letter and a shovel out to your garden, dig a hole, and bury the letter while saying, 'I release you [insert his name here] from my life'. This may not be a good option if your letter is as long as an encyclopedia.

The Men I've Almost Dated

The Ex Connection

I'm probably not the best person to give advice about how to attract and date the right men. But I have learned lots of lessons about what not to do. It's retaining these lessons that I've struggled with. But I guess that's just the process I'm going through. Sometimes we're served the same crap until we learn we should ask for something different on the menu.

Sometimes bumping into your exes will remind you just how far you have, or haven't, evolved.

Most of us harbor that wonderful revenge dream of bumping into an ex who broke our heart. In these satisfying scenarios I always look fabulously stylish and five kilos lighter. I chat in a friendly but non-committal way to the ex before I'm whisked away by an incredibly sexy new boyfriend. As I disappear into the distance my ex thinks, 'Why did I ever let her go?'

Lucretia Ackfield

Unfortunately, my fantasy revenge dream hasn't happened yet. Instead I tend to bump into exes when I'm definitely not dressed to impress …like the day I saw the Fireman.

It was one of those days when I wasn't feeling particularly fabulous. I'd done the basic minimum before leaving the house and was rushing through the local shopping centre.

It had been years since we'd seen each other and the Fireman still looked hot. Have you ever met an ugly fireman? Even the ones who might look plain in another job still look gorgeous when you know they're a fireman. They wear a uniform and rescue people. It's the ultimate combination of sexy and saviour.

The Fireman spent our brief but friendly conversation looking down at me from his great height of over six foot, grinning and looking hot (oops sorry, I already mentioned that didn't I).

I stood there in my flat shoes (when I usually wear heels everywhere!) with no makeup and old, daggy clothes while desperately wishing I could disappear. As I drove home I wondered why couldn't I

bump into him when I looked fabulous?
Sometimes life is just unfair.

I've made some interesting choices when
it comes to men and when I bump into an ex
years later I often wonder…what was
I thinking?

I had a brief fling with Mick. He was a
twenty-something who worked in my
building and told me he wanted to be a
rockstar. He also admitted that his guitar
playing sucked so it probably wouldn't
happen.

I saw him about a year later on level six.

The lift stopped, the doors opened and
there he was, seated at the reception desk.
He was still sexy but had changed his
appearance a little and, as the doors slowly
closed again, I began convulsing with
silent laughter.

Mick was fun. But we both knew he was
never going to be more than casual sex. In
hindsight it's just as well because his new
hairstyle, a green Mohawk, would have
clashed with most of my outfits.

I have some nice memories of Mick. But
sometimes your exes don't help you feel
good about yourself. Instead they remind

you of less than ideal decisions you'd rather forget. I usually behave in a rational and relatively mature way when I see an ex. I possess the required social skills to smile hello, have a chat and then move on. But sometimes this maturity takes a leave of absence. I think there will always be some people who rattle your cage no matter how 'over them' you are.

When I saw Larry and his girlfriend outside the cinemas one night, it shouldn't have mattered. Larry was the guy who constantly flirted with me in my dance classes until I found out he had a girlfriend, threw a bit of a tantrum and he apologised.

Nothing had happened since then and it was more than 12 months later. But instead of responding in a calm and mature manner I immediately lost track of what my friend was saying and fought a ridiculously juvenile urge to scurry like a frightened mouse into the nearest hole in the wall. It was a completely irrational response to seeing someone I had never dated.

Sure, if we'd made eye contact it might have been a little awkward but we probably would've smiled and moved on. And yes, his girlfriend would probably still want to scratch my eyes out but that was unlikely to happen in a public place.

But my brain just screamed 'AVOID and EVACUATE IMMEDIATELY'.

It was not my finest moment and I still don't understand why bumping into some guy I had a crush on threw me into a complete spin. I mean, not actively seeking a conversation with Larry was smart. But wanting to flee the scene like a criminal was a little over the top. And what is the likelihood of Larry, who I no longer share any common activities with and lives on the other side of the city, showing up randomly in the same location as me. Yep, in a city of more than one million people, there he was.

I guess sometimes our emotions create strange reactions and we all just act a little crazy. The lesson I learned is that I should try a little harder to act maturely when confronted with awkward situations. Or I could start wearing sunglasses and a cloak at night so I can travel incognito.

Lucretia Ackfield

The Big Ex

Seeing your ex-husband is usually awkward, even if the divorce was amicable. But the conventions of polite society will dictate you smile and pretend that being in the same room is the most natural thing in the world.

Good preparation is the key to surviving these encounters.

My first encounter with Daniel post-divorce occurred two years after we decided our marriage was over. We made the decision to end our marriage on the Australia Day weekend in 2006.

Two years later, on the Australia Day weekend, we would both attend the wedding of our mutual friends, Damien and Lily. Daniel would be there with his new partner Katrina and their newborn baby. I would be there alone; no partner in sight, just me. I wasn't sure how I would survive the experience.

The Men I've Almost Dated

I almost hired an escort; someone to go with me, look hot and generally help me to be fabulous. I wouldn't have sex with him though. Well, maybe I would if he was hot and I was drunk. Perhaps we would fall in love and live happily ever after, just like Debra Messing in *The Wedding Date*.

Of course I realised that wasn't very realistic and the online profiles just sounded sleazy so I decided to go solo. I would look as hot as possible (a strict pre-requisite) but it was my insides I was worried about. How would I cope? Would I fall to pieces? Could I smile while my ex's new life was rubbed in my face while I stood alone; fabulous but alone; successful but alone; confident but alone.

Fucking alone.

Samantha said I shouldn't go. 'Don't put yourself through it,' she advised. But Damien and Lily used to share my house and I loved them dearly. I wanted to help them celebrate their special day. I also wondered what it might cost me in the process.

I would only know a few people at the wedding. Daniel, his partner Katrina and their kids; Damien and Lily; the groom's immediate family; and another couple who had their own newborn twins.

The reception was informal and seating was self-selected. People who knew each other would naturally sit together.
I was screwed.

I circulated as much as possible before realising I could lean against the nearest wall, eating my dinner with one hand while firmly gripping my wine glass in the other; foist myself on a group of strangers at another table; or be a grown-up and sit with the people I knew.

I took the grown-up approach and walked over to where my ex and our mutual friends were seated.

We all acted normal and it was fine. But my face and brain were really hurting by the end of the night. It takes a lot of energy to act normal. I also took regular breaks and had girlfriends on speed dial. Those girls helped me keep my sanity. Being hit on by the groom's good-looking and much younger cousin also helped prop up my struggling ego. It was a long, long night. But we all made it through okay.

The Men I've Almost Dated

I chatted to Daniel and got to know Katrina better. I also met their new baby, Mandi and that was weird. I can remember looking at her and thinking, 'That's Daniel's baby'. I felt like I was having an out-of-body experience. Then I thought, 'If we'd had a child would she have looked like this one?' But I let that thought go almost as soon as it arrived. I'd never really felt the urge to have children with Daniel and that was still okay with me.

Katrina's two children were also there and seemed curious to know more about me. I found myself chatting to them too and it was all rather surreal. At the end of the night I hugged Daniel goodbye and as I pulled away, he grabbed and held my hand tightly between us, just for a moment. We looked at each other and it felt like we were both remembering everything we'd had together and lost.

Then we said goodbye, he let go, and left with his new family. I didn't see Daniel again for a few years. But this year, I've seen him twice within a couple of months.

Lucretia Ackfield

He lives with his family a few streets away in the house we renovated together but it's as if we inhabit two completely different worlds. Although we go to the same shops, cinemas and petrol stations, we never meet. But this year, I saw him at Damien's 40th birthday and for some reason I freaked out the whole way to the party and then freaked out the whole way home too.

I'm not sure why I did that. Was it was just the knowledge that we would see each other again after such a long time? Or was I feeling over-emotional, vulnerable and recently single again? Whatever the reason, we both played our 'act normal' parts as before and it was good to see he was happy.

A few weeks later, we met again as I walked home from the ANZAC Day Dawn Service. It's held a couple of blocks from my home and every year I drag myself out of bed, throw on some clothes, rub the sleep from my eyes and stumble to the war graves to pay my respects in the early hours.

I'm not at my best pre-dawn and this year, as I stepped off the curb I heard the whirr of wheels and a frantic, 'Look out!' as a bicycle and its rider emerged from the dark and almost ran me over. I jumped back onto the curb and she yelled 'Sorry!' as she passed.

I made it to the service in one piece and was walking home when a familiar voice called out, 'It's a bit early for you to be out of bed isn't it?'

I turned to find Daniel and Katrina cruising down the hill towards me on their bicycles. They'd decided to attend the service for the first time.

We exchanged a few pleasantries before Katrina made her confession. She was the rider who'd almost run me down. She said she didn't recognise it was me until she'd passed (what are the chances of that happening?). It was also far too early in the morning for me to recognise a random cyclist let alone the current partner of my ex-husband.

We stood in the post-dawn light and laughed about the incident together. It was just the three of us. It was the third time I'd seen them since the divorce but it didn't feel awkward or forced. It was comfortable and relaxed. We were just three people who shared converging histories.

Lucretia Ackfield

Katrina and Daniel are very alike; certainly more alike than Daniel and I ever were. They seem well matched too and are the kind of couple that makes sense. People can see how and why they came together.

People made such different observations about Daniel and I. 'He's not what I expected,' they would say. 'He's not the kind of person I thought you would be with.' They always expected a man in a suit not a cabinetmaker, not a quintessential Australian larrikin who would be happy to wear thongs and board shorts to every social event if he could get away with it. Maybe they were right in thinking we were mismatched.

While we stood talking, I noticed a ring on Katrina's left hand. 'Are they married now?' I thought. 'When did that happen?' But I didn't feel tempted to ask the question aloud and, as I walked away, I realised the answer didn't matter.

Somewhere during that conversation a page had turned for me. A chapter had ended. I realised I could finally move on. I'd spent so much time in the past few years feeling guilty and worrying that Daniel hadn't moved on and wasn't really happy. I'd caused a lot of pain in his life and I'd never really forgiven myself.

But that was just my ego talking because Daniel is happy. He has been for a long time and it just took me a few years to realise it. Daniel and Katrina have a beautiful little girl and they share so many interests. And that makes me really happy because I'm not responsible anymore. I'm only responsible for me.

Seeing them finally helped me let go of everything that used to be. Now I'm finally free. I'm free and ready to turn the page and start the next chapter in my life.

It's time.

Lucretia Ackfield

The Men I've Almost Dated

Epilogue

It's 2am and I'm sitting in bed wondering where the heck my thirties went.

In just over six weeks I'll be 40 and I'm not looking forward to my birthday. I haven't decided if I'm going to throw myself a party or just hide under my bed until it's all over. I know it's just another day and really, I know my life is pretty amazing right now. I'm about to finish the draft of my first book and, thanks to a redundancy package, I've spent the past year basically doing whatever I want. I'm free and independent but there's something missing.

I'm still single.

I am in love though. It's been a long time since I've felt the emotion and I like it. It's good to know I can feel that beautiful joyous love again. Unfortunately the man I'm in love with isn't in love with me. So it seems I have fallen for an unavailable man. Again.

It feels like every man who has wandered into and out of my life over the past few years should have 'unavailable' stamped on his forehead. But it's time for a change so I've written the following letter to the Universe...

Dear Universe

Please stop sending me unavailable men. Seriously, please just stop. I'm over it. I know I'm supposed to learn lessons from these experiences, but I'm not really sure what those lessons are. All I know is that every man I've been attracted to or involved with since my divorce has been unavailable.

And the range of these men has been extensive. You've certainly educated me in the breadth of this category. Here are just some of the types I've learned about...

The intimacy-challenged or emotionally messed up - these ones can't commit, aren't over their ex or they've been burned so many times they can't trust another woman.

The substance abuser - if he can't get that stuff under control, then he's definitely not available for a relationship.

The one who is too young. Duh! This is a no-brainer.

The married or already-in-a-relationship man. Note, a third party usually informs me

The Men I've Almost Dated

*about this type of unavailability as the men
involved, strangely, rarely volunteer this
information.*

*The physically unavailable. This category
includes the long-distance relationship man
and men who don't really like sex or
affection, or have issues with their bits and
don't think it's important enough to do
anything about it.*

*And then there's the 'tyre-kickers'. Just
like the man in the car yard who can't really
afford the vehicle but kicks the tyres anyway
because he wants to look like he's serious,
this man is a fraud. He will initially seem
like he's available but, once I scratch the
surface, I'll discover he's just as hopeless as
the rest.*

*So Universe, I kindly request that you
stop sending me unavailable men. They are
exhausting and I'm sick of giving my heart
to them because they only give it a good
kicking.*

*Instead could you please send me a
loving man who I'm attracted to? I'd also
like us to have some stuff in common. It
would be great if he could accept me as I am*

Lucretia Ackfield

*as well. And for God's sakes can you make
sure he can get it up!*

*Maybe you could ask Santa to deliver him
for Christmas?*

Kindest regards
Lucretia

Acknowledgements

The Men I've Almost Dated drew its first tentative breath in the mid-2000s after I recounted my latest dating disaster to my dear housemate Shelley. She turned to me and said, 'Lu you've got to write a book because you couldn't make this shit up.' Thank you Shelley.

Over the next few years I scribbled random thoughts on receipts, post it notes, in journals and on scraps of paper. But it was only when my beautiful friend Dotti (going through her own divorce) said my crazy stories made her feel more normal that I began to take it all seriously. Thank you Dotti.

Shortly afterwards the Universe dealt me a nasty blow and I found myself stuck at home every night, recovering from a painful back injury. It was time to put all those notes onto the computer. Thank you Universe for forcing me to give up my frenetic, party girl lifestyle and get organised. Thanks also to Super Puss, my tolerant and faithful four-legged companion, who kept me company for the duration.

Lucretia Ackfield

There are so many people who've helped me along the way and I cannot possibly list them all. If I have omitted you from the following list, I sincerely apologise. But please know every kind word of encouragement you offered helped make this book a reality.

Thank you to everyone who gave me support and witnessed my seemingly never-ending angst and self-flagellation during my separation and divorce (Jen, you were truly wonderful; I still think of you every time I drive past the Normanby). Thank you also to Dave and Lani, Kate, KB, Christine, Terri, Chrissy, Jenelyn and Bek.

Thank you Matt for being my writing buddy and giving me feedback on my first rough drafts (even when my stories of badly behaved men made you feel profoundly uncomfortable). Thank you Debbie, Marianna, Gert and Sarah from my writing group – you always inspire me with your literary courage. Thank you Bree for casting the very first editorial eye over my manuscript and giving me kind feedback (you were way too generous but I loved you for it). Thank you Kristy for your supportive

The Men I've Almost Dated

but firm editorial hand and for helping me to get the tone just right (I couldn't have done this without you). Thank you Hannah for creating a beautiful cover that reflects my journey (and my eternal love, stilettoes). Thank you Mum for encouraging me to publish my book (even when you didn't want to read about my sex life).

Finally, thank you to all the men I've almost dated. Your behaviour has made me feel incredulous, sad, despairing, frustrated, abandoned and ridiculous. I have frequently humiliated myself at your feet, offered you everything and received nothing, and pursued you repeatedly. I have abandoned my self-respect, acted like a petulant child and experienced epic confusion. You've helped me learn a lot about myself (some good things, some seriously wacky) and a little more about men (some bad, some nonsensical). It's been a hell of a ride but, without you, there would be no book. So thank you from the bottom of my heart. You have made this piece of literary frivolity possible and for that I will always be grateful.

Lucretia Ackfield

About the Author

Lucretia Ackfield is a writer, university tutor, public relations professional and intuitive mentor who loves nothing more than helping people uncover and share their stories with the world.

She still believes in love and explores her 'single reality' with a mixture of trepidation, enthusiasm and frustrated desire while also embracing her intuitive gifts and the unexpected insights they bring to her life. This interesting combination of professional, worldly and other-worldly experience makes

Lucretia Ackfield

for a fascinating, insightful, passionate and
witty writer with a full-frontal sense
of humour.

You can find more about Lucretia, her
words and mentoring programs at
www.lucretiaswords.com

The Madness of Love

Coming soon

THE MADNESS OF LOVE

Lucretia Ackfield

An enticing concoction of reality, fantasy
and other-worldly insight.
Can you find the line between madness
and love?

Lucretia Ackfield

Can't Let Go

A thousand scenarios play in my head
And you're in every one
Every day or so it seems
It's like I need a gun
To blast away all knowledge of you
How it felt to see your heart
And how mine felt in return
Two beating, gentle hearts

But you're not here
You're nowhere
And I am here alone
My pedicurist offers to set me up
With friends of hers back home

Still thoughts of you
They stalk me still
I cannot let you go
I love you still
You're with me still
I cannot
Cannot
Let go.

Love is a Mess

Love is a mess
I said to my friend
She agreed, nodding her head
It's disruptive, untidy and
sometimes unclean
It will completely mess with your head

First you're up
And then you're down
It's not like the fairytales
Those sweet stories didn't account
For the vagaries of male and female

And what about the pain we inflict
On the dear ones who we love
We do it so carelessly
Love doesn't always feel sent from above

Sometimes it rises from the bowels of hell
It tears your soul in two
Before the next second lifting you
up so high
And filling you through and through
With a lightness so golden
And so incandescent
You wondered how you did without

Lucretia Ackfield

All its glory and boundless joy
It turns you inside out

Then there are the errors
The plain misunderstandings
We don't know how to correct
Instead we watch our lover unravel
Sometimes not even sure what
we've said

We screw it all up
We throw love away
Even when we desperately want it
We crave another's touch
Yet turn away
We think they couldn't possibly want it

We'll go out and sleep with so
many others
Who'll never come to close
to our heart
Yet avoid talking to the one who does
For fear they'll tear us apart

We'll be struck down so maudlin
Then lifted so high
With hope coursing through our veins

The Madness of Love

Then in the next second we'll
plummet on down
And hit the dirt again

And for those who shake their heads
And say
Come now
Love is so simple
I challenge you to look at the truth,
my friend
I know that love ain't that simple

It twists and turns
Its trails unexpected
Sometimes rocky and sometimes
so smooth
Just when you think you've got it all
worked out
It'll throw you out of your groove

Roller coasters, jumps
Endless joy and succour
You'll feel like you can fly
Before explosions make you less secure
You might feel like you could die

Lucretia Ackfield

But what you learn
Along the way
Is really so very delightful
Unconditional love looks at you
And sees a navigate-able minefield
It cares not for the past
Or the challenges that have been
It sees only what is possible
The love within
The crazy impossible dream
It doesn't believe anything's impossible

It sees past your flaws
Those dents and grazes
You think are so very unsightly
Even when you feel like it's darker
than pitch
It still sees the sun shining brightly

Love is a mess
A glorious mess
And I'll take it every day
Over the safety of living without it,
my friend
You know
I'll take it every day.

Leaving Only Love

When I trace
The outlines of your scars
I see the battles you've fought
Some you've shared
And others not
But God, how much you've fought

The fragments of pain
Stuck in your skin
Taking years to ease on out
Eventually expelled out into the world
After shredding your insides out

The burdens and disappointments
They've bent your back
They've cracked the bones within
Yet now you can straighten up
And feel the light within

You worry still
About your scars
Noticeable, unavoidable flaws
Yet they have made you my love
All those nasty scores
That crisscross your soul
They've created love

7

Lucretia Ackfield

That feeling still within
The heart not yet vanquished
But beating strongly
I can see it still within

The scars they show
The lines of your journey
They show just what you've made
Of challenges, rejection and
non-discernment
All the mistakes you've made

They show the markings on your feet
Where you've walked across the coals
Just to make it to a better place
Seeking treasures still untold

I trace the outline of your scars
My fingers lightly brush
All that has been done
And is now gone
Leaving only love.

Reunion

Come to me my darling
Shrug off your heavy cloak
The one that carries pain from your past
Cast it to the moat

Leave the lead boots at the door
You know the ones I mean
They are full of disappointment
At the loss of your sweet dreams

Remove your vest
The one that's kept
Disillusion close to your chest
Hang it there beside the hat
That blocked the hopes in your head

Step inside
It's nice and warm
Defrost near the fire
Allow it to melt away the cynicism
That's frozen all your desire
Pull up that chair
That one there
And feel its soft embrace
There's no need to hide anymore
You can leave the filthy race

Lucretia Ackfield

Where you've been trying to just keep up
A semblance of appearances
When you no longer care for all of that
No more keeping up appearances

Allow your heart to slowly open
Be brave, see what's inside
Wow, so much beauty
I can see it now
I always knew it was inside

Unwrap your dreams
They haven't gone
They weren't vanquished after all
You can live them if you believe
That's called faith, after all

Open your hands from their clenched fists
Feel the warmth of mine
I'm still here
I never left
We've stood the test of time

Open your eyes
And see mine
You'll see it's not too late
The horse may have bolted

The Madness of Love

But my love
It's never really too late

Open your arms and hold me close
Breathe gently for a while
Smile at me
And make me laugh
How I've longed for your sweet smile

Take me to bed
Allow no division
Between your skin and mine
Take me there
I long for that
To feel you deep inside

Afterwards lay with me
And tell me of your heart
Of all your wanderings
Adventures and mistakes
And how we'll never again
Be apart.

Lucretia Ackfield

Culmination

Your lips on mine
Your hands they close
And embrace my cleaving hips
Your tongue it explores
My mouth so gently
My breath catches on my lips

I feel your chest
Its heart so strong
The beat it moves in time
With my own
My breasts they long
To feel your strokes in time

My hands they drift down to your waist
Your mouth it stays with mine
Your hands now underneath my shirt
My back it moves in time

I feel the curves of your hips
Then down I move much further
To your thighs
Oh man, it's so hot
I begin to explore you further

The Madness of Love

Your single hand unclips my bra
I've always loved that move
While we stand
Your hands are sure
My shirt is off
It's a single movement

Your shirt unbuttoned
Did I do that
Oh God this is really happening
My hands they feel you through your jeans
Oh yes, this is really happening

You have me up against the wall
I'm finding it hard to breathe
But, oh God, please don't stop
Who cares after all about breathing

Your mouth encloses on my breast
I'm starting to lose my vision
My eyes they close
I'm all sensation
There is no indecision

You rise again up to my mouth
Your hands caress my breasts

Lucretia Ackfield

My hands now they begin with impatience
I want you fully undressed

My hands they fumble at your waist
Your laugh rumbles deep within
You reach down to give me a hand
Then let me reach right in

I feel your cock
Oh my God
I think I'm going to faint
It's long and strong
I want it now
I definitely don't want to wait

But you my love
Have other ideas
We're going to take it slow
My clothes slide off
You know what you're doing
Of this, I already know

You descend again
You tease my breasts
With your mouth and then your hands
Then your mouth is somewhere else
My hips they seem to expand

The Madness of Love

Your tongue it finds
Your desire
My knees well now they buckle
You hold my bum
Gently close to you
But your mouth is not so subtle
You suck and swirl
I'm losing my mind
And then I come and come
They say that bucking is a cliché
But my love I bucked and then some

You return to my mouth
Your tongue seeks within
Your skin upon my skin
You find my ear
Oh God where do I begin
To describe
What's happening to me
I'm not sure that I still can
Then you pull me to the floor
And I realise I still can
Your skin with mine
No separation
It's time to go again
Your entry is strong
I pull you in

Lucretia Ackfield

I want you again and again

Your moves are sure
You want me now
But you're determined to bring me along
Your stroke is long
I'm desperate now
It's building for far too long

My hips they move now with your own
My need overtaking yours
My back it arches
I hold your eyes
There is no keeping score
You give to me and I to you
My love just what is this
We come together
Again and again
No separation
Only bliss

When we're spent
You rest a while
Your cock is still within me
I love it there
And I love you
With you, your soul completes me

The Madness of Love

You smile at me
You say my name
And I begin to cry
I've found you at last
And you feel the same
God it's taken us so much time

But no more waiting
No more hiding
No more distance or fear
You pull me close
Soon we'll go again
Our longing has no fear.

Lucretia Ackfield

The Moon and the Stars

She called for the stars
He gave her the moon
He gave 'til there was no more to give
But she didn't see
She was looking at the stars
She hadn't known how to forgive

She didn't know
Had never worked out
That the moon and the stars combine
To light up the heavens that
stretched above
And she'd had both all the time

The stars were hers
She put them
She didn't need the stars from him
But he held the moon
Which she also needed
And it was offered to her by him

The exchange though
Must be completed
There was a transaction that was involved

The Madness of Love

He would give the moon to her
While she'd give so many stars untold
Between them both they could light
the sky
And transcend the heavens above
All that was needed was real trust and love
To create the beauty above

So he stood there with the moon in
his hands
And she had her sack of stars
Could they trust enough to make
the exchange
And heal all their previous scars

She was ready
And so was he
Their hands were stretching out
It was time to leave all doubt behind
And discover what true love is all about.

Lucretia Ackfield

Never a Dull Conversation

Do you remember
There was never a dull conversation
Between us
Never
Not once

When I look back now
It's quite perplexing
How the conversation always flowed
With you
And yes
Between us

Sometimes I'd worry
About what we'd say
But then the words would flow
From me to you
And back again
Onwards and onwards they'd go

I can't imagine
You ever being
Ever remotely boring
It makes me shake my head
That realisation
Conversations without moorings

The Madness of Love

Words that flow
Wherever they like
Introspection, laughter and joy
Challenging my own reflections
Just a single boy

No not a boy
But a true man
Sorry for the mistype
It's true you're a man
The reference to boy
Just rhymed better at that point
It wasn't insight

How peculiar
To not seek for words
To fill up empty spaces
To find companionship
And connections too
In such unlikely places

Our conversations were never dull
And for that I am so grateful
I miss them now
Of course I do
I wish for them by the plateful.

Lucretia Ackfield

www.ingramcontent.com/pod-product-compliance
Lightning Source LLC
Chambersburg PA
CBHW072053020426
42334CB00017B/1488